The Ultimate Awareness, an Eternal Constant

Volume Two

Writings by the Author

The Ultimate
Prayers and Excerpts from The Word
Success Is Normal, Just Be Yourself,
   Your Eternal Identity
Fulfillment of Purpose, Volume One
Fulfillment of Purpose, Volume Two
You Are the Splendor
Gems & Poems of The Ultimate
The Gospel According to Thomas
Three Essential Steps
The Omnipresent I AM, Volume One
The Omnipresent I AM, Evidenced, Volume Two
The Ultimate Awareness, an Eternal Constant,
   Volume One
The Ultimate Awareness, an Eternal Constant,
   Volume Two

These and other books available through:
Mystics of the World
Eliot, Maine
www.mysticsoftheworld.com

The Ultimate Awareness, an Eternal Constant

Volume Two

Marie S. Watts

The Ultimate Awareness, an Eternal Constant
Volume Two
by Marie S. Watts

Mystics of the World First Edition 2016
Published by Mystics of the World
ISBN-13: 978-0692682951 (Mystics of the World)
ISBN-10: 0692682953

For information contact:
Mystics of the World
Eliot, Maine
www.mysticsoftheworld.com

Photography by © Dr. Joel Murphy 2016
www.DrJMphotography.zenfolio.com
Printed by CreateSpace
Available from Mystics of the World and Amazon.com

Contents

To The Reader

This is the second volume of the class we experienced in Vista, California in 1968. The subject of the class was, and is, "The Ultimate Awareness, An Eternal Constant." It would be most helpful to first read and perceive the Absolute Truths revealed in Volume One of this Self-revelatory experience because these are necessary as a preparation for the greater and higher revelations of the second half of the class, as presented herein.

Those of you who experienced the class will discover there are many further revelations presented in these pages that were not experienced during class.

Beloved One, these are the glorious revelations that have surged and flowed daily and hourly since the conclusion of our class sessions.

No assumptive human being—under any name—has revealed these glorious Truths or the words in which they are presented. The words have merely been heard, and now they are written. Each day and night, the revelations have been—and are—higher and more wonderful. Therefore, I sincerely hope that you will begin to read this volume at the beginning and read to the end, in order that your revelatory experience be one of ever greater joy and glory. The revelatory experience of the study and contemplation of this volume might not be complete, or satisfying, if you—the reader—at first just leaf through the book and read certain passages at random. This book is revealed for the fulfillment of a tremendously important purpose, and it is to be the fulfillment of that purpose in and as your experience.

When you are reading the following revelatory words, do not try to interpret the meaning of the words. The revelation is never in the words. Always the revelation is experienced when the Consciousness is "full open" and when there is no so-called mental effort to understand or to interpret the Absolute Truths that are merely symbolized by the words.

So, dear reader, it is my sincere hope that you will read this volume of classwork as *"full open"* Consciousness. Read in much the same way that you would view a beautiful sunset, a magnificent painting, or listen to a beautiful symphony. *The revelations will be experienced* but not by any so-called reasoning process. They will be your experience, just as they have been — and are — the experience of all who read and contemplate as "full open" Consciousness. To contemplate is to view things as they are, and never is there any mental effort involved in just viewing and seeing, listening and hearing, the glory that is God revealing Itself as the Consciousness that *you are.*

Therefore, beloved One, as you read, you will realize that *the I AM that you are* is every Absolute Truth that is so gloriously revealing Itself. It is with joy far beyond words to express that these revelations of Absolute Truth are going forth as a fulfillment of a glorious purpose in, and as, the experience of everyone, who finds this book in his hands and who reads in, and as, *"full open"* Consciousness and the infinite, boundless full open Consciousness is the I AM *that you are, that you have ever been, and that you will everlastingly be.* Go forth and stand upon the Mount, for *you are the Mount 'pon which you stand.*

Boundless Light and Love,
Marie S. Watts

Chapter I

The Ultimate Awareness
Is Absolute Perfection

But when that which is perfect is come,
then that which is in part shall be done away.
— *1 Cor. 13:10*

The Ultimate Awareness is Absolute Perfection. The Ultimate Awareness is present right here and now. Conscious Absolute Perfection is the *only* Consciousness, and the Presence of this one and only Consciousness precludes the possibility of conscious imperfection. This means that there cannot possibly be a consciousness or awareness of imperfection.

To be conscious Absolute Perfection is to be *consciously* perfect, complete, whole, immutable, constant, and eternal. In Webster's Dictionary we find the word *absolute* as being "free from limit, restriction, or qualification." It is interesting to note that the word *perfection* could be defined in these identical words. Perfection—in addition to being completely whole, immutable, constant, and eternal—is also completely free from any limitation, any restriction, or qualification. The Ultimate *is* the Absolute, even as the Absolute is the Ultimate.

The Ultimate is *now*. The Absolute is *now*. Therefore, the Ultimate is not something that must be hoped for or attained. Rather, it is a constant, immutable, eternal, consciousness of *being*. Thus, the Absolute Ultimate does not come and go, nor does It fluctuate. There can be no restricted or qualified Absolute Ultimate. There can be no temporary Absolute Ultimate. There can be no limited Absolute Ultimate. It simply is All. The Ultimate Absolute is God, and we know that God *is* All, even as All *is* God. Therefore, the Absolute Ultimate is as omnipresent as is God because *God is the Absolute Ultimate*. It is as eternal, as constant, and as immutable as is God. It is as unqualified, unlimited, and unrestricted as is God. How, then, can the omnipresent, omnipotent Absolute Ultimate fluctuate? How can It come and go? How can It appear or disappear? It cannot. And It does not begin nor does It end. Neither can It ever be any more or any less complete Perfection.

The Absolute Ultimate is constantly the Presence. This is true, even though we may seem to be unaware of this fact. The Bible states it so beautifully:

> And it shall come to pass, that before they call, I will answer; and while they are yet speaking, I will hear (Isa. 65:24).

And the glorious Omnipresence that is the Absolute Ultimate is clearly stated in Jeremiah 23:23:

> Am I a God at hand, saith the Lord, and not a God afar off?

And of course, all of us are familiar with that beautiful reassurance as given in Psalm 139:7-8:

Whither shall I go from thy Spirit? Or whither shall I flee from thy presence? If I ascend up into heaven, thou art there: if I make my bed in hell, behold, thou art there.

Yes, the Absolute Ultimate—which is absolute, eternal, constant Perfection—is everywhere because It is *the* Everywhere. It is the Consciousness of this fact, and of being this fact, that is the power of the Absolute Ultimate Truth.

Oh, beloved One, let us be through with futile imaginings and vain hopes for attaining Absolute Ultimate Perfection. Let us be through with the misconception that someone called teacher, leader, master, etc., has attained this glorious, conscious awareness but that we have yet to reach such heights. No one "attains" the Absolute Ultimate Perfection— every Identity *is* this Absolute Ultimate. And no one can attain the Absolute Ultimate Perfection because the Ultimate Perfection is that which he eternally constantly *is*. Let us freely and fully acknowledge and admit that we are "the fullness of the Godhead bodily" and that we are "complete in him, which is the head of all principality and power." This is clearly and succinctly revealed in these quotations found in Colossians 2:9-10.

Any attempt to understand or to analyze the meaning of the statements of Truth you read or hear will only seem to delay your full and complete consciousness of this Absolute Truth and of *being* this Absolute Ultimate complete Perfection. This is true because such an attempt is a denial of the fact that you already are the Intelligence that knows the Absolute Truth and that knows Itself to *be* this Ultimate Perfection. Any effort to interpret the statements of Absolute Truth you read or hear is based on an assumption that you are not already conscious, or aware, of what it means, and all that it means. Thus, you would seem to be restricting or limiting your own consciousness of the Absolute Truth and of *being* this complete, unrestricted, unlimited, Absolute Truth.

The boundless, infinite awareness of being the very Presence of every Absolute Truth—infinite Perfection—that you are is never realized through self-denial, self-limitation, or self-restriction. There can be no qualified acknowledgment and acceptance of this Absolute Truth. Your Consciousness must be "full open" and with no reservations concerning Its being an absolute, unqualified Truth, or Fact. In short, it is necessary to go all the way in the acceptance of the glorious Fact that Absolute Perfection is already here, all that is ever here, and all that can ever be here, or anywhere, and that this Absolute Ultimate is what you are, all that you are, and *only* that which you are.

Absolute Perfection is not something that is yet to come. Neither is It something that is yet to be revealed. Absolute Perfection is that which is *now* constantly and eternally here. Furthermore, It is all that is here; It is all that has ever been here and all that will ever be here. When we read or hear statements of this ever-present, omnipresent, Absolute Perfection, we do not reason or ponder about the meaning of these statements. Neither do we try or make an effort to understand or to interpret these statements. Never do we attempt to analyze them. To do this would mean that it was necessary for us to try, or to make an effort, to know that which we already are and know our Self to be. It would also mean a denial that we are completely conscious of that which we *already* are conscious of and conscious of being.

When we gaze upon a beautiful sunset, into the glorious Heart of the rose, or upon anything that is perfect and beautiful, we never attempt to interpret, to reason out, or to analyze this perfect Beauty. Rather, we are just "full open" Consciousness, considering the absolute, perfect, omnipresent Beauty that is revealed. When we behold anything that is absolutely perfect, it would never occur to us to reason or to ask why this Perfection is so perfect.

In like manner, when we read these wonderful statements of Absolute Ultimate Perfection, we do not analyze, try to interpret or to understand the words. Rather, we simply rejoice in just considering the Absolute Perfection that is being revealed. We are aware of the fact that this Ultimate Perfection already *is* and that we are the Consciousness that is aware of this Truth and of being this Truth.

Truly, "that which is perfect is come." The Absolute Ultimate Perfection is here, now, constantly and eternally. This Perfection is revealed, and It is revealed right now in and *as* the "full open" Consciousness that you are. Beloved, you are the Perfection that is being revealed, and you are the absolute, perfect Consciousness that is revealing Itself *as* Itself. In short, you are the revelation and you are the Revelator. Consider these glorious facts.

Truly, "that which is in part shall be done away." All the former seeming misconceptions of duality, of twoness, of otherness, is done away. All assumption that there is God but that there is also something or someone other than God *being* is transcended. As "full open" Consciousness, you stand. Beyond all the duality of formerly assumed metaphysics, you stand. Far beyond all apparent darkness, or ignorance, you stand as full, complete, enlightened Consciousness. The Light *is*, and you are the glorious Light that is and is All.

> The night is far spent, the day is at hand: let us therefore cast off the works of darkness, and let us put on the armor of light (Rom. 13:12).

Beloved, the "works of darkness," of ignorance, of duality, are "cast off." The Consciousness of *being* the Light—complete Absolute Perfection—reveals the glorious fact that always, eternally, constantly, we have been this Light which is complete, conscious Perfection. Always we will remain this Light. Never were we in darkness. Never were we actually aware of duality or ignorance.

That which we have always known, we know now. That which we have always been and will forever be, we are *now*.

Chapter II

The Beginningless, Changeless, Endless, *I* That I Am

Throughout the ages, there has been much curiosity and much concern as to what happens when that which is called death seems to overtake us. But the primary concern seems to pertain to just what takes place after this assumed experience.

There is a wonderful answer to these questions to be found in *The Gospel According to Thomas*. (Right here it must be stated that I do sincerely hope you have a copy of the above-mentioned book. This book presents 114 authentic sayings of Jesus, and in these statements you will find the Absolute Ultimate Truth beautifully revealed.)

In this glorious, revelatory book, we find the disciples questioning Jesus about what the end—or that which they consider to be the ending—of their life will be. But Jesus makes it clear that so long as they have not discovered what they consider the beginning of their life to be, they cannot possibly know what the ending will be. Jesus well knew—and knows—that in order to know that Life does not end, it is essential to know that Life does not begin. This knowledge, of course, means that it is necessary to be aware of the fact that there is neither birth nor death. Furthermore, Jesus makes it exceedingly clear to the disciples that the so-called beginning and that which is called the ending are one and the same illusion. This, of course, means that neither so-called birth nor death has anything to do with the eternal Identity that exists as each one of us.

Jesus then continues with the exposure of the fallacy of birth and death. He clearly states that those of us who stand — despite any appearance of birth — firmly aware of *being* beginningless and endless Life are indeed blessed and that we are to perceive that there is no death. Then he tells the disciples — and all of us — how blessed are those who continue to be aware of what we were and what everyone and everything was — and is — before the death called birth seemed to overtake us.

Indeed, the *I*, or Identity, that you are and that I am can never begin, change, or end. The uncreated Identity that is the I AM that you are can never cease to be. This I AM has not changed into another identity. Neither has this I AM — nor can this I AM — be any more or any less aware of being complete — but specific — as the Identity that All eternally, constantly are. This Identity, I AM, has never been, nor can It ever become, anything other than the *I* Identity that It is. This *I* Identity eternally *is*, could never begin, and could never cease to be.

If sickness, imperfection, change, age, or deterioration could exist now as the substance of the *I*— Identity — that you are, they must always have been, and thus will ever be, the substance of the I AM that you are. Furthermore, if these so-called opposites of the God I AM—that you are—are here now, they are everywhere, infinitely and eternally. Thus, there could not be an atom, a nucleus, or a cell anywhere that was not ill, imperfect, changing, aging, deteriorating, and even dying. Needless to say, every atom, nucleus, cell, or whatever in existence consists of Consciousness, Life, Intelligence, Love. And of course, this conscious Life is God Being That.

If there could be an item, aspect, of this Substance—Body—that was absent or missing, it would have to be forever missing. This would mean that you would eternally exist as an incomplete identity and an incomplete substance. In like manner, if there could be a vacuum in or as the Substance in Form that is here now, there would have to be a vacuum in or as the Substance that is Infinity. Thus, we would have an incomplete Universe. Of course, this would be impossible because this boundless Universe is God, and it is inconceivable that God, the All, could be incomplete.

Infinity and Eternity are one and the same. Here and now are one and the same. There can be no "there." There can be no "then" or "when." Nothing comes and nothing goes. Nothing begins and nothing ends. All, everything, *forever* is. Everything and everyone is an eternal, infinite Constant. There is never more nor less of anything or anyone.

For instance, Vision is eternal, constant, infinite, immutable, complete—and *you are that Completeness.* The Vision you are never began, never came into being, nor can It ever end, or cease to be. The Vision that you are is never more and never less. It is as immutable as is the I AM that you are.

Hearing is an eternal, immutable, infinite Constant. The infinite Hearing that you are is never interrupted. It does not come nor can It go. It is never any more, nor can It ever be any less. It is constantly and forever immutable, complete, and you are That.

The Mind (Intelligence) that you are is indeed eternal Intelligence. It does not come and go. It never begins nor does It ever end. It is never any more, nor can It ever be any less, intelligent. The infinite, eternal Intelligence that you are is everlastingly, constantly immutable and complete. It is a *universal Constant* without limits, divisions, or restrictions. It can never change. The Mind (Intelligence) that you are remains forever constantly, infinitely, eternally complete, and this complete Intelligence consists of all knowledge, of all that is known and of all that can be known. *Only that which is Absolute Truth can be known.* This is the all-knowing, all-being, Mind (Intelligence) that you are. And this, Beloved, is the all-knowing, all-being Mind, Intelligence, that *you* are now.

If any Absolute Knowledge were missing, or absent, from the Mind that I am—and that you are—right here and now, infinite, eternal, constant,

21

complete Mind (Intelligence) would have to be incomplete. In short, Intelligence would be filled with vacuums. It would have to be absent from Itself. This is true because Mind (Intelligence) is a universal, constant Existent. In fact, Mind, Life, Consciousness, Love, *is* the very Substance that comprises the Completeness that is this Universe.

There can be no vacuums in Infinity. But neither can there be a vacuum in Eternity. Of course, there can be no vacuum in Omnipresence. Actually, Omnipresence and Constancy are the same, for Omnipresence is constant, even as It is all that is ever present. The I AM that you are is not a vacuum in the midst of the universal Light—all knowledge—that you are or that I am. Rather, the I AM that you are and that I am is the Completeness that *is* the Light. All is Light, and there is no darkness for the I AM that you are to be. Indeed, the all-knowing Mind (Intelligence) that you are *is* Light, and in this Light—complete knowledge—there is no darkness at all.

Often we hear someone speak of knowledge as Light. He will say, "Oh, now I see the light." Or he may say, "I am completely in the dark on this subject. Please enlighten me." Well, *knowledge is Light*. And if we were to supply a name for darkness, it would have to be *ignorance*, or absence of knowledge. Again, we would have to accept a vacuum in Mind, Intelligence, Light. But actually, *all is Light*. So all is complete Intelligence; thus, all is complete knowledge.

The foregoing statements lead right back into our ceaseless theme, namely:

> No one can teach any Truth to us that we do not already know, that we have not always known, and that we will not everlastingly know.

This, of course, is true because Intelligence is equally intelligent as each one of *us*. Consciousness is equally conscious as each one of us; Life is equally alive as each one of us; and Love is equally loving as each one of us. Living, conscious, loving Mind (Intelligence) is Infinity, or God, and we know that God is equally present as each one of us and as all that comprises the infinite variety that *is* this complete Universe.

This, Beloved, is what we mean when we state that there is never more or less anywhere of the universal Presence which is God. In 1st John 1:5, we read:

> This then is the message which we have heard of him, and declare unto you, that God is light, and in him is no darkness at all.

Indeed, God *is* the complete, All-knowing Intelligence in which there is no ignorance, no incompleteness, and no absence of complete Intelligence. Thus, God *is* Light, and because God is all there is for us to be, we have to be the Light, which is God, and there can be no darkness in the I AM that we are. How could we be anything that God is not, when *God is all there is for us to be*?

23

This is why we are the Light in which there is no darkness. This is why we are uncreated, beginningless, changeless, and endless—deathless. We can no more begin than God can begin. We can no more be created then God can create—or recreate—Himself. We can no more change than God can change; and we can no more end or die than God can end or die.

Truly God is All. Truly All is God.

Chapter III

Consciousness in Action

Consciousness in action is effortless Activity. In order to be aware that you exist, the Consciousness you are has to be active. Consciousness in action is your awareness of being. Consciousness in action is your awareness of being alive, intelligent, loving, and it is even your awareness of being conscious. But this also means that your awareness that you exist is actively conscious of being Life, being alive, of being intelligent, of Love being loving, and Consciousness being conscious.

This awareness of being necessitates activity. It requires no effort to be aware that you exist. Yet as just stated, your consciousness that you exist must be active in order for you to be conscious of being. Omniactive Consciousness of being is eternally, constantly aware of being. But it is well to perceive the absolute Fact that Consciousness is also Substance. In fact, *Consciousness is all Substance, all Activity, all Form.*

From the foregoing statements, it is clear that your very omniactive Consciousness that you exist is your *only* Substance. Furthermore, this same awareness of being is the Substance, Form, and Activity of everyone and everything that you see, hear, are aware of, or know. Yes, Consciousness is your Awareness of being, but Consciousness is also the very Substance, Activity, and Form of that which you are aware of being.

A complete comprehension of these facts will mean a completely effortless activity in and as all of your experience. Every aspect of your daily experience will be effortless activity. But this is not all. Every bodily activity will be free, perfect, and without any strain, fatigue, or effort. Oh, it is wonderful to be aware of the unconcerned freedom of activity we experience, and experience being, when we realize the complete, omniactive nature of the Consciousness we are.

Is there any difference between the activity of your Consciousness that you are alive and the activity of your Consciousness that you are aware of walking, talking, breathing, etc.? No! There is not one iota of difference between your Consciousness actively aware of being and your Consciousness of being any activity. This is true of *any* bodily activity, even as it is true of any activity of your daily experience. But Consciousness, Mind (Intelligence) Life, Love are all one and the same. This is why Consciousness in action is always intelligent activity. It is conscious Intelligence, or intelligent Consciousness, in action. Conscious Intelligence is constantly in motion, but the activity is always intelligent activity. This is why all of your activity is so perfect.

Omniaction is just as constant, just as omnipresent, as is Consciousness, Life, Intelligence, and Love. But

Consciousness in action is also Omnipotence. The All, the Only, the Totality that *is*, has to be the only Power there is. Only that which is present is, or can be, Power. An absence could never have or be Power.

You can see that it requires no effort for Consciousness to be in motion, or to be active. (It is well to frequently remind your Self that Consciousness — or conscious Intelligence — is the *only* Substance; thus, the only Substance that can act is intelligent Consciousness.) Consciousness does not resist being active. Neither does It limit Its activity. Consciousness does not complain. It does not ache, pain, or become weary, despite the fact that It is constantly, eternally in action. What does it matter whether we walk one mile or five miles? There is no resistance to our being active; thus, there is no awareness of making any effort. How, then, can there be any fatigue, weariness, exhaustion, etc.? How can there be any depletion of strength, when it is all conscious Omnipotence in action? The Consciousness you are simply walks, acts, lives, breathes, etc., with no awareness of that which is called time or space.

Consciousness in action is irresistible, non-depletable, and irrepressible. It acts of, and as, Itself. We do not compel infinite, omnipotent, intelligent Consciousness to act. We do not even direct Its activity. Being intelligent, It knows what It is and what Its activity is. Consciousness is fully aware of just what Its fulfillment of purpose is, and It is continuously, actively fulfilling Its purpose in being. This is true whether this Substance—Consciousness—is called the heart in action, the lungs, liver, or whatever. Where we seem to have problems is through our mistaken misconception that we must do something about this perfect activity.

Intelligent, living Consciousness is weightless. It is not an awareness of heaviness or of solidity. Its awareness of being active has nothing to do with a non-existent, supposedly born body of matter. It is never divided by the delineations in, and as, which It evidences Itself. For instance, there is absolutely nothing about the delineation of Consciousness called the Form of the Body that divides or separates the infinite, omniactive Ocean of Consciousness. Therefore, the Body can no more be—or become—weary, burdened, or fatigued than can the infinite Light which is Life Itself.

Sometimes someone will say, "I become mentally exhausted to the point where I can't think anymore." Well, right in these words is the answer. Whenever we *seem* to become mentally tired, it is always because we have been trying to think; we have been making a mental effort. We have seemingly been attempting to supplant Mind—infinite Intelligence—with a supposedly "thinking" mind.

This all-knowing Intelligence never indulges in a thinking process. Mind always and constantly knows. Conscious Intelligence does not have to think in order to *know*. Awareness is all knowledge, and this awareness is constant, ever-present, and eternal. It is inconceivable that living, intelligent Consciousness would have to think in order to instantly know whatever was necessary to know at any moment.

It is supposed to require some so-called mental effort in order to think, but certain it is that no effort is required in order that Consciousness be aware of any necessary knowledge. Conscious Intelligence is complete, and this Completeness *is* all knowledge. "Full open" Consciousness never thinks. It never concentrates in meditation or in any thinking process. Rather, It contemplates, or considers, the knowledge that is being revealed as the Consciousness of the Identity. It is all so very simple and so effortless.

So, beloved One, you can know without effort. You can live, move, *be* the Substance which is Consciousness, Intelligence, effortlessly being constantly active.

This does not mean that we never experience. On page 85 of *The Gospel According to Thomas*, Jesus makes it clear that omnipotent, omnipresent Omniaction is evidenced as Man by a "movement" and a "rest." This is Absolute Truth. There truly is a movement and a rest. But the rest is never complete inactivity. There is no such thing as complete inactivity. We can symbolize the movement and the rest by the tides of the ocean as they come and go. All of this perfect activity takes place in a rhythmic pattern, or design. The ocean does not become inactive when the tide is receding. Rather, it is just a balanced, rhythmic, intelligent, effortless activity. It appears to move forward and then to move backward. It is a definite fulfillment of purpose. But the movement is neither forward nor backward. It is all the irresistible, swirling, surging, circular movement of the ocean eddying—in and as the infinite ocean of conscious Omniaction.

To us it may appear that we rest when we sleep. This is true. But we *never* become completely inactive. During that which we call the sleeping period, Consciousness would have to become unconsciousness in order to be completely inactive. If Consciousness were to be without any activity, it would mean so-called death. In some of the earlier writings of the Ultimate, I have discussed that which is called sleep, so I shall not repeat that which has already been revealed and written. But it is well to occasionally contemplate the fact that Consciousness in action is intelligent, effortless Omniaction.

Chapter IV

Music Is Substance

Donald Hatch Andrews, in his book entitled *The Symphony of Life*, reveals very clearly the fact that music is the Substance of Infinity. And this is true. In many aspects of illumination, we hear the Music of the Spheres, and it is indeed a glorious experience. This Universe does consist of Music. This is why some of us often hear this music when we are experiencing illumination. But to continue with our subject, Music *is* Substance. It is the Substance that comprises this Universe. So you see, Substance can be heard, even as Substance can be seen. The hearing and the seeing are the same thing. It is all Consciousness.

In India, there is an enlightened one whom they call The Mother. She states that the appearance of the body, including every organ, cell, atom, nucleus, etc., is but the symbol of the actual Energy which does exist, and she points out that this Energy exists in innumerable forms. There can be no doubt but that this one is exceedingly enlightened. But from the standpoint of the Absolute Ultimate, the symbol, if such there were, would have to consist of the very same Substance that comprises that which she calls the Energy in innumerable forms. (This is no criticism of this great one.) Nonetheless, if there is such a thing as a symbol of the ever-living Light—Energy—the symbol and the Light would have to be one and the same indivisible Substance. Otherwise, we would have to accept the duality of Energy and something separate from, or other than, the Light, or Energy, which is actually the living Substance in Form that *is* the Body.

All that can really be called an appearance is anything that appears to be imperfect, inharmonious, or temporary. But the Perfection evidenced in Form that we call the Body *is real*. It exists. It is genuine. It actually exists as eternal, changeless, constant, absolute, perfect Substance in Form. This Substance is Consciousness—God—manifesting Itself as just what God *is*. So the Body is the manifestation, the *evidence*, of the absolute Fact that God is.

Now, I am not speaking only of the Substance in Form called your Body. Rather, I am speaking of *any* Substance in Form, and as I have so often stated: *all Substance is in Form.* Even every nucleus, every so-called atom, every so-called cell, exists in, and as, Form, and it matters not whether it is evident to us as tree, rose, bird, blade of grass, or whatever—it is the eternal, uncreated Light in Form.

We know that Perfection is complete Beauty and perfect harmony. We also know that Music is Beauty and perfect harmony. But Music is also Form and perfect, rhythmic Activity. So Music is Substance, Form, and perfect, rhythmic Omniaction, and this Substance is Consciousness, God, manifesting Itself as just what God is. Certain it is that there is nothing solid, dark, dense, or immovable about Music — *but It is Substance*. This being true, it follows that every aspect of *any* Form — no matter what it may be called — is constantly present as this Body, as the Body of everyone and everything that exists. It is small wonder that some of the astrophysicists are now saying that the universal Substance is Music. Of course, the glorious fact of this revelation is that Substance in Form is not separable; neither is It solid, dense, dark, or inactive. Always, *Substance in Form is perfect, harmonious, eternal, constant, and beautiful.*

Music *is* Substance. It is the Substance that comprises this Universe. So you see, Substance can be heard, even as Substance is seen. As we have often stated, the seeing and the hearing are one and the same. But by this same token, all art is Substance. We gaze at a beautiful painting, and we are inclined to consider it as though it consists of so-called material canvas, paints, in various forms and colors. But actually, this painting consists of the same Substance that is Music. *There is but one Substance*, although this one indivisible Substance is evidenced as innumerable rhythms, forms, colors, etc. It is all Consciousness, Life, Intelligence, Love.

The innumerable "bodies" of Light, Life, Energy which comprise this Body are present right here and now. This Body is alive, so Life is here. It is conscious, so Consciousness is here. It is intelligent, so Mind is here. It is loving and lovely, so Love is here. There is nothing solid, dense, dark, or material about Life, Consciousness, Mind, or Love. Yet it is true that this Substance in Form can and does evidence Itself as Substance in Form that can be seen. It is visible. But it can also be heard speaking or singing as the voice or even as someone whistling or as a whisper. We can also hear the movement of someone walking, etc. Oh yes, we can hear this seemingly invisible Substance in many aspects of Itself. Never do we associate that which we hear with solidity, density, etc.

Now, since the hearing and the seeing are identical, why should we consider that which we see as being material? We can perceive this Truth, and once it is completely revealed, we know that the Substance in Form that we see really is the supposedly invisible Light, Life, Consciousness, Mind (Intelligence) that is all Substance. Therefore, you see, this Body can indeed evidence Itself constantly, eternally. Thus, the Light—Life—that comprises this Body is Power. It is the Power of being Its own evidence of—and as—Itself.

In music, the tone, the pitch, the various rhythms, the activity, does exist. They exist as one integral, indivisible, complete Whole. They exist as the ever existing Truth, or Fact. This Fact is the so-called Energy that is Power, being infinite, yet right here, right now, constantly and eternally. The I AM that we are is the Power to read or to write any note, sign, etc., that indicates, or signifies, the Presence of any tone, pitch, rhythm, or rhythmic tempo. Why is this true? It is a Fact because *we* are the Life, the Energy, the Light, the Principle which is Music Itself. Of course, this same Fact is true of, and as, every painting and every work of art.

This same Fact is true in mathematics. The mathematical Fact, or Truth, exists. Otherwise, the figures could never be written or read. We are the Power to instantly write or read the figure that signifies the presence of the Principle—mathematics.

Now, we should clearly realize an exceedingly important point: we may speak of the notation in music or the figures in mathematics as symbols which signify music or mathematics. In a sense, this is true. But *the symbol is not something else, or other than, the Music or the mathematical principle.* That which may be called the symbol has to be the Principle, the Substance, Form, etc., evidencing Itself. It is *all* Consciousness. It is Consciousness visibly and audibly evidencing Itself, even as the musical notation or as the mathematical figure. There is nothing other than Consciousness that can evidence Itself. There is nothing but Consciousness that can be the evidence of Itself.

Beloved One, in considering these Truths, it would be well to perceive that these Facts are true of—and as—all visible or audible Substance in Form. In short, that which may be called the symbol of the tree actually *is* the tree Itself. If the tree did not exist, the evidence of the tree could not be seen. If there were no such thing as tree, there could be no visible evidence of tree. The so-called symbol, or visible evidence, is never something separate from, or other than, that which is being manifested, or evidenced. (Neither can the visible evidence of this Body be something other than, or separate from, the actual living, loving, intelligent Consciousness in Form that is this eternal Body.)

The Music that is signified by the notes cannot be altered. It is constant, immutable, eternal. It cannot be touched or invaded. It remains intact, immune, as just what It *is*. This Fact remains, even though the symbols may *seem* to be imperfect, distorted, or absent. *Absolutely nothing can ever change, alter, or erase even one single sonata, song, or symphony.* The everlasting, *specific* symphony, sonata, etc., is an eternal Constant. As stated before: the Music is complete harmony, and harmony is Absolute Perfection. It is perfect, eternal, constant, living, intelligent, conscious Love Itself. It does not do anything—It simply *is*. And just by being, It evidences Itself as just what It *is*, and nothing else.

What is it that hears the Music before the symbol is written? Is it not the very same Consciousness that writes the symbol? The hearing of the tones, etc., and the writing of the symbols are simultaneous. This fact is particularly evident when one is improvising at the piano. The hearing of the tone and the touching of the key, signifying the presence of the tone, are simultaneous. It is Consciousness that hears the tone. It is Consciousness aware of being Music that is conscious of *being* the tone that is signified. It is this same Consciousness that touches the keys and that writes the notes that are called symbols. Therefore, you can see that the tone, the key, and above all, the Music, are one and the same thing—it is all the Substance in omniactive Form that is called Music. The seemingly invisible Perfection, harmony, rhythm, and forms that comprise Music *is* the presence of the Power that can—and does—manifest Itself as perfect evidence. The symbol of itself cannot be either perfect or imperfect. Actually, it is the Presence of the Perfection that is the Music that acts, and the Activity of this Presence—Music—is manifested as the perfect evidence, or symbol, of Itself.

Now, one might ask whether or not the note that signifies the Presence of the Music is necessary. (It is true that some of us constantly hear Music, but this does not seem to be the case with all of us.) Indeed, the notation that signifies the Presence of the Music is essential at this point. It is necessary at this particular phase of our existence, but once we constantly *hear* the Presence that is Music, we are aware of It in, and as, Form, color, Substance, and Activity. It actually is visible and audible.

It is in this same way that this so-called symbol called Body is necessary just now. It has to be visible, even as the notes that signify the Presence of the Music must be visible. If this were not true, Jesus would not have presented a visible image of the Christ that he was—and is. Jesus knew that this visible image, called Body, was necessary in order that he fulfill his purpose in being. (Incidentally, whenever it is absolutely necessary, right today, Jesus does appear visibly to those who recognize the ever-presence of the Christ.) In any event, there had to be something that was hearable, touchable, visible to those who apparently could not, at the moment, see, hear, or touch the Substance in Form that really was—and is—the eternal, constant, changeless Body of the Christ. As we have stated earlier, Jesus said, "Having eyes, see ye not? and having ears, hear ye not?" (Mark 8:18). He also made it very clear that even though we seem to be blind, we actually do see.

Chapter V

The Significance of Paul's Illumined Experience

Why was it that Paul seemed to be blind after his walk and talk with Jesus? It had to be this way because otherwise Paul might have seemed to lose, or to have forgotten, the genuine Vision of things as they are and as they were seen during his walk with Jesus. Paul might very well have accepted and believed the misperceptions as he *seemed* to see them, "through a glass, darkly." And it is when we seem to see through the eyes of supposedly born man that it appears we see through a glass, darkly.

Thus, Paul had to experience this period of seeming blindness in order to clearly perceive, thus see, that the apparently invisible things—Substance in and as Form—could really be seen, heard, and touched. Yes, the God-conscious Awareness that is the eternal, birthless Christ-Man can, and does, really see, hear, and even touch the genuine, perfect everlasting Substance in Form that *is*.

Suppose Paul had believed that his blindness took place because he actually saw and heard Jesus and because he walked and talked with Jesus. Suppose he had blamed the glorious, illumined experience of this episode for his apparent blindness. (Some individuals do this, you know.) But if Paul had misunderstood why he seemed to be blind, he would still appear to be blind.

Was the apparent blindness of Paul evil? Not at all. Paul had to see all things as they genuinely are. Thus, he had to see as the Vision that is infinite, boundless, birthless, deathless, eternal. Could the Vision be called evil? Not at all. In order that Paul truly *see*, he had to appear—for a little moment in the eternality of his existence—to be blind. Thus, the apparent blindness was not evil. Rather, it just signified the Presence of the Vision that *is*. And of course, this signal was Good, or God, in action, evidencing Itself.

Suppose Paul had believed that his apparent blindness was caused as a punishment for sins of omission or commission? For instance, he could have believed that he was being punished for his persecution of Jesus and those who believed in the Christ. He could have even believed that he was suffering because of some sin he had committed in a supposedly former lifetime and that he was working out his karma.

Well, if Paul had been deceived by any of these delusions, he would have missed the glorious significance of his experience in walking and talking with Jesus; thus, he would have gone right on apparently paying the terrible price for sins he had supposedly committed *Oh, where is the omnipresent Love that is God in such a great cruelty?* Never could there be sin and punishment. Neither can there be such a monstrosity as a law of karma.

What was—and is—the one called Paul? Is he now, or could he ever have been, other than the very Presence of God, being the Christ—the Father being the Son? Could there ever have been, or can there be here and now, a Life that is alive, a Consciousness that is conscious, a Mind that is intelligent, a Love that is loving that is not God? Is not the *only* Christ —thus, the *only* Man—simply God evidencing Itself? God, being God, aware of being just what God is, is the Christ, the Son, Man.

It was no mere happenstance that Jesus was suddenly visible and hearable to Paul. Nothing ever happens haphazardly or by chance. Always, in every episode or experience, there is a definite and specific purpose to be fulfilled. Thus, there was indeed a purpose to be fulfilled by Paul's experience. This purpose was fulfilled and is still being fulfilled today. For instance, consider the many Absolute Truths presented in the sayings of Paul as revealed in our beloved Bible. Jesus, the Christ, does manifest himself to us, even as he did to Paul, whenever there is a definite purpose in his being visible and audible. Then it is that we realize that Paul's illumined experience is also our illumined experience, and the purpose of this experience is fulfilled.

Of course, it is true that later, Paul did seem to revert to the so-called born man level, even though he had experienced this great illumination. But don't we also sometimes *seem* to drop back into darkness, even though we have experienced glorious illumination? At least for a while, we seem to fluctuate. However, when Paul seemed to descend from the heights, he did feel that he had to organize the glorious Absolute Truth that had been revealed as he walked and talked with Jesus. Nonetheless, we do recognize the fact that the churches—organizations—have fulfilled, and some of them are still fulfilling, a definite purpose. If it should be that they no longer fulfill any purpose in being, they will cease to be.

However, if Paul had remained at the height of his illumination and had continued to "see" as the infinite Vision, he would be visibly walking in and as the Body of ever-living Light which he genuinely is. It is not surprising that Paul appeared to drop back into darkness. As we have stated, this same mistake seems to be our experience. We do seem to temporarily return to darkness—ignorance. We appear to feel that we just have to have a leader, a master, or a teacher. Some of us feel that we must belong to a church or a religious organization. Yes, even after we have reached the heights of Heaven, we may seem, for a while, to descend to the darkness of supposedly born man, Nonetheless, we do arrive at a point beyond this seeming return to ignorance—darkness. We ultimately do arrive at a constant awareness of seeing, thus being, the glory that is the Entirety of all being and of the I AM that we are. In short, we actually do see things as they are. We perceive that "Seeing *is* Being." Above all, now we know:

> We are that which we see as the Infinite Vision seeing.

Behind and beyond every so-called descent into seeming darkness, ignorance, blindness, there *is* the Light. Behind and beyond every seeming inharmonious event, episode, or experience, there really is the forever constant Light, revealing and evidencing Itself as just what It *is*. The darkness is nothing of itself. It only signifies the Presence of the Light. It only focuses our full attention upon the Light that is here. The Light *is*. The seeming darkness is not. Neither can it be because God, the All, the *Only*, is Light. And our Bible clearly states that in Him there is no darkness at all.

Beloved, *you are the Light, and nothing else or other than the Light exists as the I AM that you are.* You are the Light, in whom "is no darkness at all." This is the God I AM that you are, here, now, eternally and constantly.

> Walk ye in the Light, as the Light, for you are the Light in which you walk.

As you contemplate this Absolute Truth, you will surely perceive—and experience being—every Truth you are perceiving.

Chapter VI

The Purpose of the Symbol

Previously we have discussed the symbol. Now we have an opportunity to consider this subject, and there is more to be revealed pertaining to that which is called the symbol.

There are some who do not like this word *symbol*. To them, it appears that the symbol is something separate from, or other than, the infinite, indivisible God I AM Consciousness. But of course, there can be nothing that is separate from, or other than, God. The symbol does exist; it is the visible and audible evidence of the Truth it symbolizes. The very same Consciousness that is the Absolute Truth images Itself *as* that which It symbolizes. Now, let us explore this subject of symbol in greater depth.

We might ask, "Is the symbol conscious of being?" All existence is Consciousness, and Consciousness has to be more than merely conscious. In order to be conscious, It has to be conscious *of* something. We have often stated that whatever we are conscious of, we are conscious *as*. This means that whatever we are conscious of, we are conscious of *being*. Certain it is that we are conscious of the symbol; therefore, we are conscious of *being* the symbol. Yes, we are aware of being the very Form, Substance, and Activity that is the symbol.

The symbol is the visible evidence of the Principle of that which it symbolizes. We have said that the note symbolizes the Principle which is Music. We have also said that this Universe consists of Music. Thus, a full and complete awareness of infinite Music, sometimes called the Music of the Spheres, is indeed important. In order to be aware of the Music of the Spheres, we have to actually hear it. This is the Music that we hear when we are hearing with "that other ear" that Jesus mentions in *The Gospel According to Thomas*. As we now know, Music does exist as Substance, Form, and Activity. It exists as color, order, and balance. It also exists as every rhythmic tempo that *is* this omniactive Universe. So an awareness of this Principle, Music, and of *being* Music Itself is of paramount importance.

Let us now return to our subject, which is "The Purpose of the Symbol." The symbol is the visible, audible, and touchable evidence of the Principle. For instance, in Music, the existence of the notes, etc., is entirely dependent upon the Consciousness of the one who hears, plays, or writes the musical symbols. The symbol does exist as Substance, Form, and Activity, but this visible evidence has to be the Consciousness that evidences Itself as the Substance and Activity called the symbol. Only in this way can the symbol be anything.

It is our Consciousness of being that evidences Itself as the symbol. It is in this same way that our awareness of being is visibly and audibly evident as the symbol called Body. Of Itself, by Itself, the Body—symbol, visible evidence—could not exist at all. Of or by Itself, It could know nothing. Neither could It do anything. The symbol—Body—cannot act of, or by, Itself. Yet It is active. However, this Activity is the God-Consciousness, the I AM, acting as the Activity of the symbol—Body—or the visible manifestation of the awareness of *being* the I AM. Therefore, this Body has to be the perfect evidence of the *I*, or I AM—the Consciousness of being. This is true because the eternal, constant, conscious I AM *is* the Principle—Perfection—Itself. Perfection has to evidence Itself as what It is. So the symbol, visible evidence, of the Perfection that is, is the awareness of perfect being, evidencing Itself as Perfection.

But suppose one should *seem* to temporarily descend into darkness, ignorance. Suppose one should seem to weaken, to become only partially conscious or even completely unconscious of being the eternal, constant, immutable Perfection that is. If anyone could appear to become unaware of the God I AM, it could seem that the visible evidence—symbol, Body —of the God I AM could appear to be blotted out and thus seemingly obliterate the ever-perfect Body that *is*.

This superimposition can seem to assume a presence, a power, and an activity of itself, by itself.

Oh yes, it can even assume that it is in control of itself, that it has conditions, problems, pain, imperfections, etc. But it can even pretend that it is born—begins—must mature, change, become aged, deteriorate, and end, or die. It can even appear to have the power of itself to mesmerize itself to the point of complete obliteration. This pretense of existence can seem to appropriate to itself the power of sickness or health, life or death.

Of course, actually none of these horrendous things can happen. It is utterly impossible for the I AM to really descend into darkness and ignorance. It is only a "seeming." Nonetheless, it can appear to be genuine, or an actuality. But the I AM that I am remains intact and completely immune to any seemingly distorted symbol or imperfect, inharmonious, visible evidence.

As it so often happens, when we have—in our contemplation—realized a great height as the Light, we find ourselves ecstatically saying:

> Right here, now, eternally, constantly, I am awake. I am the control. I am the Power. I am the order and the balance of the ever-conscious *I* that I am. I know what I am, I *am* what I know. Thus, I constantly, *consciously* manifest the eternal, constant, changeless Perfection that I am. I am aware of being the ever-perfect, eternal, immutable symbol—visible evidence—of the *I* that I am.

> Right here, right now, constantly, infinitely, and eternally, I am the visible evidence of that

which I am, of all that I am, and *only* that which I eternally, constantly am.

If the artist is fully aware of *being* the art, the Beauty, which is being symbolized as the painting — the visible evidence of this art — this Beauty is Perfection Itself. But if he seems to be unaware or only partially aware of *being* this Beauty, it can appear that an imperfect symbol — painting — can be manifested. Yet inevitably, the artist continues to attempt to perfect the symbol. He will erase or paint over and over the seemingly imperfect evidence of the Beauty that he actually sees and *is*.

Now, the Beauty that is the perfect picture existed before the artist even began to paint it. Actually, this beautiful image has always existed and will forever exist. Had this Beauty not already existed, the artist could not have been conscious of it. Had this Beauty not been already present in and *as* the Consciousness of the artist, he could never have perceived its existence as that specific picture. Oh yes, the artist always "sees" the picture before he begins to actually paint it.

Now, the artist is aware of the fact that the perfect Beauty that he sees can be manifested. It is manifested as the glorious Substance, the color, the balance, the order, the rhythm that comprise the perfect symbol — manifestation — of the Art that *he* is. Thus, he is aware of the perfect symbol — visible evidence — called the finished painting. But, beloved

One, this perfect, visible evidence is not perceived so long as the artist continues to *try* to reproduce the picture he sees in something he may call his "mind's eye." Neither is the perfect Beauty attained through an attempt or effort to improve the symbol or painting. It is rare indeed that an artist is satisfied with his painting, a composer is satisfied with his compositions, or an author is satisfied with his writing. This is true because, generally, the artist is *trying to reproduce* a picture of the Perfect Beauty that he sees, or the composer or author is *trying* to reproduce the Beauty of the Music or of the poem or literature that he hears. From this fact, it is apparent that the artist already knows that the perfect picture has to exist because he has already seen it before he began the painting. But the Beauty that is the picture is evident when the artist does not make any effort to reproduce the picture that is already present within and as his Consciousness. He simply lets the Beauty that is his own Consciousness, and that is the picture, evidence *Itself*.

When the artist is aware of *consciously* being the symbol, visible evidence, of the Beauty he is seeing, the visible evidence is as perfect as is the picture he has been seeing all the while. Now he makes no effort to make the symbol any more perfect than he already knows it to be. This is true because he is aware of being the Perfection, of being the Art, of being the Beauty, *as* the symbol. Jesus the symbol is but the visible evidence of the Perfection he is aware of being. Yes, the artist is even conscious *as* the visible evidence which is the painting.

Now, it is evident that this simile pertains to all forms of that which is mistakenly called "creative" art. So-called man is never a creator, nor is he ever a composer. How can there be an assumptive man who creates anything, when everything in existence is eternal, beginningless, and endless? Since God is not a creator, it is impossible for assumptive man—if there were such a man—to be a creator. What can man be that God is not since God is all there *is* or can ever be?

Now let us perceive the Absolute Truth that is revealed as the painting, the artist, and the art when this same Truth is manifested as the visible evidence of our being called the Body. Let us perceive that when we are aware of *being* the symbol, the visible evidence called the Body, we really see and experience being the perfect, changeless, beautiful, eternal Body. Even as does the artist, we seem to keep right on trying to improve the symbol called Body. We know the Absolute Perfection that is all Substance, Form, and Activity does exist. Yet we seem to entertain an imperfect, or incomplete, awareness of the fact that it really *is* this Body, Thus, we tend to make an effort to *improve* this evidence of our Being.

First, we may have appealed to the medical profession for help. We may have tried diets, pills, and exercises in an effort to make this perfect evidence *become* more perfect than it eternally is.

Then we may go a little higher and try to produce an improved or more perfect Body through metaphysics or through "mental work." Often, up to a certain point, this method will be helpful. But never does it go far enough. Never is the eternal, constant, changeless Body revealed and experienced until *all* duality is transcended and we are aware of *being* the evidence of our existence *as* the perfect Body Itself.

It is noteworthy that the artist can improve the symbol—painting—to a certain degree. He does this by making an effort to reproduce a more perfect painting of the Beauty that he sees. But it is the same dualistic method that we seem to use in metaphysics. We also can, up to a certain point, seem to improve the *symbol* of the perfect Substance in Form that we perceive ourselves to be. Yet all the while, this Absolute Perfection which we are striving to portray remains intact and immune to any attempt we make to perfect that which is already perfect. We can never improve Perfection. We can never make Perfection be any more perfect than It eternally, constantly *is*.

Now let us see what is necessary in order that the symbol—visible evidence, Body—be seen and experienced as the Perfection that we genuinely are. It is only when we are aware of being the very Substance, Form, and Activity that *is* the symbol that this Absolute Perfection is evidenced as the visible and experienceable Body Itself. Beloved, the symbol—visible evidence—that *is* this Body will be completely evidenced when we are completely aware of being the Perfection that we are, manifested as the *only* Substance, Form, and Activity that is visibly evident as all there is as this Body.

Chapter VII

The Apparently Unseen Is the Seen

What is the difference between that which is seen and that which appears to be unseen? There simply is no difference at all. They are totally one and the same Essence, Form, and Activity. That which is apparently seen by the eye of man actually does exist. Furthermore, when it is seen as it genuinely *is*, it is recognized to be identically the same Substance, Form, and Activity that had appeared to be unseen

The only seeming difference is in the way we appear to have been seeing and interpreting the Substance, Form, and Activity that has always been this Body right here. It is a misinterpretation of the omniactive Substance which is in Form that makes It seem to be something other than that which It really is. But when our awareness of that which *is* is complete, this omniactive Substance in Form is seen completely, and It is seen as It constantly, eternally is.

It is that which seems to be unseen to so-called born eyes that is the Power. This is true because that Substance, Activity, and Form that appears to be invisible really is the *only* Substance that *is* present. Now, that which is present has — or is — the Power to manifest Itself visibly as *all* Substance, Form, and Activity. Our mistaken, imperfect, incomplete way of seeing things has absolutely nothing to do with the actual Substance in Form that we are viewing. Furthermore, our misinterpretation of that which we are viewing does not, and cannot, alter or distort in the least that which we are viewing. And the *Fact*, or Truth, of the perfect, eternal, constant immutability of that which we are viewing *is the Power*. Yes, the Power lies in the fact that All remains exactly what it is—and nothing else—infinitely, eternally, constantly and immutably.

The only thing that can even *seem* to change is *our way of seeing, interpreting,* that which exists right within our view. Absolutely nothing exists that can change that which does exist into something that does not exist. This, Beloved, is why it is so futile to attempt to change seemingly imperfect substance into perfect Substance. Absolute Perfection can never be any more, or any less, than that which It eternally *is*.

There is no substance, form, or activity in an apparently imperfect way of seeing things. There is no power in an imperfect way of seeing that which is forever perfect. There is no presence, thus no power, in an incomplete vision of things as they actually are. Actually, *all that is visible evidence, called the Body, is the seemingly unseen, perfect, conscious, living, loving* Mind (Intelligence) *that really is the only Substance.*

Here, again, we can ecstatically state:

I am aware of seeing and being just what I am and nothing else. Whatever I am conscious of seeing, thus being, I am aware of seeing and being right here, now, constantly, eternally. And I am aware of being that which I am seeing as this Substance in Form and this Activity called the Body. This Body is only the eternal, constant *I* that I am, fully aware of being the perfect evidence of the Perfection that I am. Yes, the Body is the God *I* that I am, imaging Itself.

The foregoing does not mean that there is any little so-called born being here visualizing itself. Neither is there such a thing as a born being to visualize itself as a perfect body. Actually, there is no born being here that can visualize anything at all. There is only God, aware of being God and aware of being God alone. This Body *is* the temple of the living God, and It is not a temporary receptacle for a so-called assumptive born being. The Lord is in his holy temple. Of course God is in this Body because God *is* this Body. Yes, God is in this Body, *as* this Body. The Body Itself *is* the temple.

It is not surprising that Jesus said, "For ye are the temple of the living God." Indeed, this is true. The ever-living God-Consciousness that you are really is the eternal temple — Body — consisting of the God I AM that *you* are. Whose Body is this? It is God's eternal embodiment of Himself. God is eternal, complete, whole, constant Perfection as all there is of this holy temple. Yes, this is the holy temple because it is wholly, completely the Substance, Form, and

Activity which is God being. And this, Beloved, is the God I AM that *you* are.

Now, it seems necessary to clarify one important aspect of the subject we have been considering. Wherever there is Substance in Form—and Substance in Form is everywhere—there is Body. As stated in former writings, the astronomers often speak of the stars and planets as bodies. For instance, they will mention the body of the planet Mars or Venus or any other planet or star they are discussing. We could speak of the body of the nucleus, the body of the atom, the body of any so-called cell, or any other aspect of this Body. And, of course, we could speak of the body of a grain of sand, of a rose petal, of a leaf, a tree, or whatever.

Therefore, when we mention the omniactive Substance in Form called the Body, we are not merely speaking of this Body. Rather, this same Truth pertaining to Body is the Absolute Truth as the Substance in Form that exists as any Body. Actually, the Universe is the boundless Body of Infinity, and of course, this is God Itself. But it is also the Consciousness that *we* are.

Always, however, we must be aware of the fact that this universal, boundless, infinite Body is indivisibly *one Body*, and although the Bodies that comprise this one indivisible Body are innumerable, there is never a separation between Bodies. Never do we return to the fallacy of dualism.

In Ephesians 4:4, we read, "There is one body, and one Spirit." And in the sixth verse of this same chapter we read, "… one God and Father of all, who is above all, and through all, and in you all."

Now, of course, we do know the genuine meaning of these verses. There really is one indivisible Body, and this Substance in Form is Consciousness, or Spirit. But this Infinitude does consist of God, revealed and identified as innumerable Identities, and every Identity is revealed and evidenced as that specific aspect of Itself called the Body. This Absolute Truth holds true whether we are speaking of the Identity called the grain of sand, the so-called cell, atom, nucleus, or whatever. The Identity is the Body, even as the Body is the Identity, and never in all eternity can there be a separation between the Identity and Its evidence of Itself as Substance in omniactive Form. If the Body could deteriorate and finally disappear, there would be a separation between the Identity and the Body which the Identity evidenced. But now we know that the Body has to be as eternal and as constant as is the Identity. This inseparability is absolutely necessary. Why? Because the absolute, inviolable Truth is that God — the infinite Universal All — is eternally, constantly, indivisible One.

Every Body in existence is a focalization of the universal, inseparable Body. You see, it is all the same Substance in Form, but It exists in Form only as the evidence of Itself. But we must realize that the existence of the Body, evidencing Itself, is the evidence of a specific fulfillment of purpose. *Everything that exists is evidenced for the fulfillment of some specific purpose.* There is not one purposeless nucleus, atom, cell, so-called organ, or whatever that is not the fulfillment of some definite purpose. There is not one grain of sand, not one star or planet that is not evidenced as omniactive Substance in Form and that is not the fulfillment of the specific purpose for which that particular Body exists. So, beloved One, the Body—whether this Body or the Body of anyone or anything—is absolutely necessary for the complete fulfillment of purpose, which is God, Infinity, eternally being the fulfillment of *all purpose.*

Chapter VIII

Distinction, but No Separation

There is but one indivisible, eternal, constant Substance. There is no Substance that is different, or other, than this one All-Substance. There is distinction, but there is no separation. The distinction between the tree and the pebble has its entire basis in the specific rhythmic tempos that are being focalized.

The physicists know this to be true. They know that the Universe — all that It is — consists of the same Substance. But they also know that the only thing that makes a rose be a rose or a bird be a bird is the specific rhythmic tempos that are focalized as the activity of the bird or the activities of the rose. Of course, all of these innumerable rhythmic tempos are infinite Substance in action, or Omniaction.

Now, some of the astrophysicists are saying that all there is of this Universe is activity acting as various and innumerable rhythmic tempos. However, there can be no activity, and certainly no rhythmic tempos of activity, unless there is *Something* that acts. Now, what is it that acts? What is it that controls, balances, and governs Itself as each perfect, specific rhythmic tempo? It is *Mind*, Intelligence, infinite Consciousness, acting intelligently. This omniactive, intelligent

Consciousness is every rhythmic tempo. It is this same intelligent Consciousness that controls and governs Itself in and as perfect order, balance, and Absolute Perfection.

Mind (Intelligence) is conscious. *There can be no unconscious Intelligence.* So Mind is conscious. Consciousness is alive. And living, intelligent Consciousness is also Love. This is why we are one indivisible One, and it is also why we remain forever absolutely perfect and harmonious. So this Substance in action is Life, Mind (Intelligence), Love, governing, controlling Itself perfectly, intelligently, and lovingly. But the Activity is not something that is separate from, or other than, the Substance that acts. The Substance is the Activity, even as the Activity is the Substance. And the Substance in Form is determined by the specific rhythmic tempos that are focalized as that specific Substance in that specific Form.

No doubt you are familiar with the chapter in *The Omnipresent I Am* entitled, "The Universal Ocean of Living Light." You will recall that in this chapter it is revealed that the Universe consists of infinite varieties of circular activities and that they resemble the eddies, or whirlpools, we observe in rivers, etc. We know these eddies may appear to be very large or small, and many appear to be moving in these circular patterns in an infinite variety of rhythmic tempos. For instance, the water in some eddies will move at far greater speed than in other eddies. This fact has great significance for us because it is these infinities of rhythms, or rhythmic tempos, that determine whether the specific Substance in Form is called a tree, a dog, cat, flower, star, planet, or man. From this fact, we can determine just how indivisible and completely impersonal all Existence really is.

In order to completely perceive just how it is, and why it is, that there is distinction but no separation, it is necessary to perceive the complete Nature of the universal *Ocean of Living Light*. We now know that this boundless Light is Substance being omniactive and Omniaction being Substance. We also know that the distinction of each Identity is determined by the rhythmic tempo of the activity of each specific Identity. Now, recalling the fact that Omniaction is Substance and Substance is Omniaction, we can realize that the various specific forms are determined by the innumerable variety of rhythmic tempos.

There may be some question as to how it is possible for Activity to be Substance and Substance to be Activity. Before the following statements are made, it must be exceedingly clear that I am not referring to a supposed born material body. *There is no matter as such; thus, there can be no body consisting of material atoms, cells, organs, and the like.* Above all, it must be clear that all Substance in Form consists of omniactive Consciousness. Always we should perceive the salient fact that all Substance is Consciousness, and Consciousness can never be — or become — materialized.

If there were no omniactive Consciousness, there would be no living Substance at all. Now let us see how it is possible that distinct forms of omni-active Substance exist, yet the distinction of the Form does not mean any separation of the one infinite, indivisible, omniactive Substance, which is this Universe. Of course, we are speaking of God. What other than God exists that we can speak about? Nonetheless, we will speak in the words that are being used by the physicists who are so sincerely exploring the Nature of all Substance in Form.

Any trained musician will tell you that if a metronome is set at a certain tempo, it acts as that specific tempo and no other. If the performer wishes to play or sing at another rhythmic tempo, he merely resets the metronome to another specific tempo. But there is always that steady rhythmic tempo, no matter at what point the metronome may be set. The tempo may be very fast, or it may be very slow, or anywhere between prestissimo, adagio, or largo. But so long as the metronome is set at that specific tempo, the rhythmic tempo remains the same.

The Activity of the infinite Substance that *is* this Universe consists of an innumerable variety of rhythmic tempos. As so often mentioned, everything in existence moves and acts as some specific rhyth-mic tempo. Yet the universal, overall rhythmic tempo is never separated by various specific tempos. There really is one overall universal rhythm. The rhythmic tempo of everything that comprises this Infinity is necessary to the completeness, the totality, of the one indivisible, overall rhythm. But the specific rhythmic tempo is also necessary to the fulfillment of purpose of that particular Substance in Form. The overall rhythm that is mentioned here is the boundless, universal, steady, changeless rhythm which constitutes every distinct rhythmic tempo of each and every specific omniactive Substance in Form.

Let us now consider this Body right here. The physicists know that It consists of innumerable atoms and that these atoms are active at various rhythmic tempos. These atoms are supposed to comprise the various cells of the Body. It is said that the cells of the heart are distinctly those specific cells and not the cells of that which is called the blood, the liver, etc. (Incidentally, I don't even like to write these misleading words.) Now, the cells of the heart are active at a distinct rhythmic tempo; the cells of each so-called organ of the Body are said to act at a distinct, specific rhythmic tempo. Yet there is an overall rhythm of the Body which determines the fact that this is the Body called man and not the Body called tree. Furthermore, the Body is one inseparable Whole, and the numerous, distinct rhythmic tempos do not separate this Body into bits and particles. For instance, we are supposed to breathe at one specific tempo; the pulse is supposed to beat at one specific tempo; and the activities of the various organs (so-called) are said to act at other rhythmic tempos. So it is apparent that this bodily activity consists of many and various rhythmic tempos.

Now let us consider the Body of the tree. The rhythmic tempos of this specific Substance in Form are also many and varied. The rhythm of the seed is that particular rhythm. Oh yes, the seed is just as eternal, beginningless and endless, as is the tree itself. The rhythmic tempos of the ever-active roots are specifically those omniactive rhythms. The trunk acts at its distinct rhythmic tempo, and the leaves are active at specific tempos. Of course, the blossoms and fruits, if the tree blooms or bears fruit, are active at specific tempos.

There are many similes we could mention, but we feel that it is now clear that it is the rhythmic tempo of each and every aspect of existence that determines whether this specific Substance in Form is an atom, a cell, a heart, a hair, or whatever. It is also clear that it is the rhythmic tempos of the tree that determine the fact that it is a tree and not grass, bird, or any other aspect of omniactive Substance in Form.

The necessity now is to perceive that the specific rhythms that are active as the omniactive Substance that is the entire tree do not divide the tree into separate bits and parts of itself. It is in this same way that everyone and everything is active and exists as its own distinct rhythmic tempos. Yet the Omni-action that is infinite is not divided, even though various rhythmic tempos determine the identity of each and everyone and of everything in existence.

What is all this Substance in Form that acts as innumerable rhythmic tempos? It is Consciousness. It is the omniactive Substance which is Consciousness existing as innumerable, specific, distinct — but inseparable — Identities. It is this same omniactive Substance — Consciousness — which is the universal, boundless Infinitude. And no matter how innumerable, are the various specific Forms that are acting at innumerable rhythmic tempos, this universal Totality remains forever inseparable.

Oh, beloved One, the name for this inseparable Oneness is Love. This is Absolute Truth in which there is no duality. This Absolute Truth in which there can be no twoness and no otherness is One alone, and there is no other.

I know that we have used many nonsensical words here; I also know that words can be misunderstood. But you will not misunderstand these words. You know that every word that could signify Substance, Activity, and Form really means God, Consciousness, Intelligence, Life — Light — and above all, Love. God truly is All. All truly is God. Yes, even that which we call Omniaction is God, for God is omniactive.

There are not two Consciousnesses. There is but One and this One is God. There are not two separate ones who are conscious of being. There is but One conscious of being, and this One is God. But you are conscious of being — of existing. Therefore, you have to be conscious of being as this one awareness which is God aware of being. God is aware of being eternal, constant Perfection. There can be no awareness of being imperfect because God — the only Consciousness — is aware only of being just what God *is*. And *you*, being this same awareness of being, can only be aware of being just what you *genuinely are*. But this is not all. There are not two awarenesses of being, identified. The only Consciousness of being identified is God, aware of being God as this specific Identity. But this is *your* awareness of being the specific — but unseparated — Identity that you are.

If we see a tree, the tree is that specific tree and no other. There are not two trees that are completely alike. That tree you see is just as much a specific Identity as you are a specific Identity. This fact is also true of a specific rose, a specific bird, or pebble on the beach. Yet, as you now know, there is not even one separate Identity. The infinite, eternal, constant, omniactive, Omnipresence that is God is ever inseparable. This is true no matter how many specific Identities there are, and as you know, these specific, inseparable Identities are innumerable.

Now, God is aware of being each and every Identity. But each and every Identity is aware of being what it is. The tree is aware of being that specific tree; thus, it is aware of being its own Identity. In like manner, the cat knows that it is a cat, but it also knows that it is *that* distinct, specific cat. And I can assure you that the rose knows that it is a rose and that it is *that distinct, specific rose.* (I have had too many glorious experiences of Oneness where trees, roses, cats, blades of grass, etc., are concerned to ever doubt that every aspect of Infinity knows that it is a distinct Identity and knows just what this Identity is.)

Jesus well knew — and knows — that the Identity remains distinctly *that* Identity, despite the fact that It exists as the one inseparable, omniactive Substance in Form. He knew that the very same Consciousness that is God, Infinity, and which is your Consciousness, is conscious as the tree, the cat, the bird, and all that exists. There is a statement in our Bible which clearly reveals his awareness of this important Truth: "And he said unto them, Go ye into all the world, and preach the gospel to every creature" (Mark 16:15). Certain it is that the word *creature* means every Identity, and, as Jesus knew, to preach the gospel to every creature means to recognize the distinct Identity that *is* each specific one and to present this Absolute Truth of Oneness.

There are many who are aware of being this *one* indivisible, conscious Life where pets are concerned. And there are some who are aware of the fact that a flower, tree, etc., is the same inseparable Consciousness — and equally the same — as are they. There is no problem of communication with any creature, whether it be man, bird, tree, flower, or whatever, Of course we don't talk about this because it sounds utterly ridiculous, even perhaps idiotic, to those who do not understand or do not experience this Oneness. Nonetheless, I must tell you that there *is* communication, and this communication is the one indivisible, conscious, intelligent, living Love speaking, or preaching, of Its awareness of *being One*.

It is true that generally this communication is not audible or in words. It is just an awareness of the true meaning of Love. For instance, I know what the rose feels when I cup it in my hands and hold it to my face. I know what the tree feels when I say, "I love you," and when I caress its trunk. Oh yes, I *know*. However, it is true that our pets often answer us in audible voices, and we need not hear any unnecessary words in order to know what they are conveying.

Yes, there is definite proof of the inseparable Oneness of *all* Existence. And beloved One, when this glorious Absolute Truth is thoroughly known, there will be no more wars. The lion *will* lie down with the lamb, and they shall beat their swords into ploughshares, as is promised in the Bible.

Of course, this is not a promise of the Heaven yet to come. Rather, it is a statement of the Heaven that is already here. It is a statement of the Heaven that has always been here and that will forever be here. But there is right now an ever greater awareness of this Heaven and of being in this Heaven, and above all, of *being this Heaven itself*.

Jesus was—and is—so very aware that the kingdom of God *is now and here*. For instance, in *The*

Gospel According to Thomas, he makes this very clear. Here we find the disciples asking Jesus when the kingdom of God would come. And Jesus plainly told them that it would not come so long as they looked for it or expected it to come at some future time. Rather, he told them that the kingdom of God is *right here,* but they did not see it.

How great is this Truth! The kingdom of God is eternal and constant. It is always here. But so long as we imagine that it is to be present some future day, we are overlooking that which is always right here. We are denying the very Omnipresence that *is* God, and this very denial will seem to postpone our awareness of the Kingdom—Consciousness—that is God. Furthermore, it will seem to postpone our awareness that *we* are the Kingdom—Consciousness—that is God right here and right now.

Oh yes, there are many statements in our beloved Bible that reveal an awareness of the presence of this kingdom of God—Heaven—that is here. All of us have read these beautiful and true statements. For instance:

> Know ye not that ye are the temple of God, and that the Spirit of God dwelleth in you? (1 Cor. 3:16).

And in Mark 1:15, we find him saying:

> The time is fulfilled, and the kingdom of God is at hand.

Oh, Jesus revealed the kingdom which is always here in so many statements. And in the 139th Psalm, we hear that inspired and enlightened David singing:

> If I ascend up into heaven, thou art there: if I make my bed in hell, behold, thou art there.

David was indeed very aware of the indivisible, infinite Presence of God being everywhere. In fact, he knew that this kingdom of God was — and it is today — *The Everywhere*. Wherever God is — and God is everywhere — right there is His kingdom — Heaven.

This fact, Beloved, is why — even though we may imagine that we are in hell — right where we are, God — the God I AM that we are — *is*. Thus, it is *not* hell. It has to be Heaven. But could it be Heaven if there were any separation, division, between the galaxies, the stars, planets, between men, animals, etc.? No! But once the duality of "twoness," or otherness, is transcended, we do discover the ever-present Omnipresence which really *is* Heaven. Best of all is the glorious fact that we discover we are in Heaven, and *we are Heaven itself*. Now, this moment, we know this is Truth. Now we *are* every Truth we know.

No supposedly born identity can compel himself to see, to perceive, thus to *be* Absolute Perfection. God, who *is* every specific Identity, is alone responsible for seeing, thus *being*, the Absolute Perfection that God is. This means that God is responsible for being this Absolute Perfection as every Identity in existence.

And God can only see — thus *be* — the Absolute Perfection that *is* each and every Identity.

Does this mean that God can be — and is — the Identity but that the Identity is not the very Existence that is God? Not at all. Rather, it means that God being the Identity is the Identity being God. Thus, the God I AM Identity is the I AM God Identity. And this I AM Identity is responsible for being just what It *is*. Nonetheless, it is true that no assumptive, little born "I" can compel itself to perceive, or to be, the Absolute Perfection that *is* already, constantly, eternally the only Identity. And this only Identity is the God I AM *I* being.

It is futile to struggle or to make any mental effort to be, or to become, the absolute, perfect I AM that we already are. Actually, this is what we were attempting to do when, in metaphysics, we were trying to solve some seeming problem or to become more perfect than we believed ourselves to be. Oh yes, we did realize some so-called healing, and we are grateful. But always it seemed there was some problem in need of healing. Thus, the mental struggle became a constant daily experience, and finally some of us arrived at the point where all of the mental struggle simply did not solve the seeming problems. Then we were compelled to be more completely aware of the infinite Identity that we were — and are. But bear in Mind that we did not compel ourselves to arrive at this point. Rather, it was the God I AM Consciousness asserting Itself as the Identity that is God being the only *I*. Thus, It is the only *I*, or Identity, being God.

The God I AM, in order to be complete, entire, total, must be the Absolute Truth—Completeness Itself. This Completeness has to consist of *all that God is, thus, all that we are.* Being just what God is, the God *I*, that *we are*, must be complete, total, entire awareness of what we are, all that we are, and *only* that which we are.

Let us be completely through with this thing of trying so hard to be or to become that which we already are, that which we constantly and eternally are, and that which we can never *become*. Never can we *become* the absolute, complete Perfection that we really are. Never have we ceased being this Perfection, and never will we begin to be this complete Absolute Perfection.

Despite any seeming problem, let us simply refuse to attempt to "work it out," or to "work our way out of it." To do so is to seemingly delay our complete awareness of *being* that Perfection which we know ourselves to be. This is true because to make an attempt to "work out" a problem means to honor the seeming problem, to acknowledge and admit that it is present and that it is *our* problem. So long as we honor and claim *any* specific appearance of imperfection, lack, or inharmony of any nature, we are going to continue to seemingly be victimized by one apparent problem after another.

Now, of course, comes the question: "But what do I do?" Nothing. But we do *perceive* something. We simply perceive the fallacy of trying to heal some apparent illness or to change some supposedly inharmonious situation. Thus, we simply admit, acknowledge, and *honor only the Absolute God I AM Perfection* that does exist and that is all that can exist. We admit that we are the Presence *only* of that which is eternally, constantly, immutably perfect and harmonious.

We don't *try* to do this. Rather, we just let go. No matter how persistent or serious any situation may seem to be, we are totally unconcerned about something that *seems* to be but is not. We simply say, "What does it matter? What is this to me? I know what I am, and I am the Perfection that I know my Self to be." And we drop the whole seeming argument right then and there. Let it go. You don't even know anything about such a fallacy. What consciousness could you be that was not aware of being complete, eternal, constant Perfection? Certain it is that you are not going to make an effort to be unconscious of something that does not exist. Furthermore, if any inharmony did exist, it would have to be infinite and eternal. What hope of ever being completely free and harmonious would there be if imperfection of any nature could be known or could exist? None whatever.

Now we can joyously say:

I am completely aware of being the presence of Absolute Perfection because I could never be aware of an absence of this complete Perfection. I am Completeness Itself. I can only be aware of being the presence of all the perfect Substance, Form, and Activity that is necessary to the complete Perfection that I eternally am. I am ever new. I am constantly new. Constant newness is the very Essence of the Totality that I am.

Thus, I am the Principle—constant, perfect, ever new Completeness Itself. This I am specifically. This I am infinitely. This I am now. This I am eternally. This I am constantly. This I know my Self to be, for I am that I AM.

Fred Hoyle, who is one of the greatest of the astronomers, has said that the heavens will always be seen just as they are seen today. He states that this is true despite the fact that every star and every planet is constantly moving. Then he gives his reason as to why the, heavens will always appear just as they do now. This explanation is very interesting, as it reveals just why we are ever new yet the same. Mr. Hoyle states that even as every star and planet moves on, there is always another star or planet right there that is already taking its place.

It reminds us of the constantly moving, boundless Ocean of living Light. The Light that is delineated as every so-called "eddy," or Form, is constantly moving, surging, and flowing on. Yet the ever new Light—Life—is constantly right there, even as the Substance is surging and moving. This, Beloved, is why this delineation of eternal, infinite, omnipresent, perfect Substance called the Body is ever new, yet ever the same.

Chapter IX

What Is Matter?

All that appears to be matter is but apparent ignorance, unawareness, of the Truth that God is All, All is God. The Substance that is delineated in and as Form that is visible to us may *appear* to so-called born eyes to be dense, dark, solid matter. But this is only the way it appears to a false, or incomplete, sense called vision. The appearance of solidity, density, darkness is not that which we are actually seeing or experiencing. The seeming solidity called matter is only our ignorance of that which is visible right here. When we actually *see* the Substance that is visibly here, we do see Substance in Form, but we do not see solid matter. And this is not all. Once we experience *being* that which is here, as the genuine, visible Substance that *is*, we have no awareness of solidity, density, or darkness. This means that we have no awareness of weight. Consciousness, Life, Intelligence, Love comprise the *only* Substance that is visible and experienceable. Living, conscious, intelligent Love is completely weightless. *But it is visible.*

This Substance that *is* can never deteriorate. This is true even though it may *seem* that deterioration is taking place or has taken place. That which seems to be deterioration merely signifies that the genuine, imperishable Substance that *is*, is asserting and revealing Itself. This, of course, only means that a more complete awareness, or knowledge, of the eternal, immutable, constant Substance that does exist is being experienced and evidenced. Actually, it is God, the I AM that *you* are, being so aware of what God is that apparent ignorance, unawareness, simply dissolve. A simile of this fact could be that of the clouds dissolving and revealing the ever-present sun.

Never do we need to be healed. All that is ever necessary is a more complete awareness of that which we already are. Furthermore, it requires a sure and certain knowledge of God. This means that we are to know what God is, where God is, and *all* that God is. We must actually *be* the full and complete knowledge that God is Omnipresence, Omnipotence, Eternality, Constancy, etc. But we must also perceive that we can *only* know that which God knows; thus, we can only *be* that which God is. We have to be the very Substance which is God in order to be aware of being any Substance at all. Thus, instead of a necessity for healing, the thing necessary is a greater knowledge, awareness, of being just what God is and nothing else.

In this awareness, the apparent ignorance, or incomplete awareness, is transcended, and we clearly perceive the actual Substance that *is*, rather than seeing, or believing in, something called matter, which is only an incomplete way of seeing things. Thus, the apparent ignorance called sickness, age, etc., simply dissolves. You see, it is in the perception of what God is, and *all that God is,* that we know—and are aware of being—just what we are. And to perceive, or to be aware, is to *be* that which we perceive. Thus, the absolute, eternal, constant Perfection that *is*, is revealed and evidenced. And often this is called a healing.

Beloved, previously I have stated that if you wish to see Man, see God as God actually is. Now let us go further with this statement. In order to see God as God *is*, it is necessary to see Man as Man is. Conversely, in order to see Man as Man *is*, it is necessary to see God as God truly is.

Ignorance, of itself, is nothing. It can only *seem* to be an absence of knowledge. But it appears to be present as though it were a material substance and activity. However, an absence, or ignorance, of something is not the Presence of that thing.

Certain it is that an apparent absence of knowledge of something that does exist could not be the Presence of the Substance that *is*. Thus, all that really is ever present is the Substance, Form, and Activity which is complete knowledge, or awareness of Being. This, of course, is the Substance that is Consciousness.

What mind exists and what mind is focalized here that is not complete knowledge? What intelligence (mind) or what consciousness exists that is not complete, perfect knowledge, or total awareness of being? It is true that every trouble, every so-called problem we seem to encounter or experience, is due to an apparent ignorance, or absence of knowledge. But it is well to perceive the fact that this *seeming* absence of knowledge is only an *apparent* absence of knowledge of what God is. But of course, it is impossible for us to be ignorant of what God is. Thus, it actually is impossible for the God I AM that we are to be ignorant of what we are. How could infinite, intelligent Consciousness possibly be unaware of being what It is and of all that It is? We know it is not possible.

All that is called evil, sin, sickness, death, etc., is but an apparent absence, or seeming ignorance, of the fact that there really is nothing that is not God being. And of course, this would also mean that it seemed that the Identity was unaware of being just what God is and of only that which God is. This is why there really is no sin, no evil, no trouble or inharmony of any kind.

But awareness of being cannot be awareness of *not* being. Awareness of being what God is cannot be an unawareness of being what God is. After all, we are totally a Consciousness of being just what God *is*, and this, of course, is God conscious of being Itself. So it is that God, the All, aware of being, is the only Substance, Form, or Activity that anyone or anything can possibly be. Thus it is that there can be no material substance in Form, and neither can there be so-called matter in action. There really is no matter to be or to be active.

That which seems to be invisible here—although it is not—is truly the Mind, Consciousness, that is God, knowing what God knows, thus being what God is. That which seems to be visible here—but really is not—is only ignorance, or apparent absence, of Mind, Intelligence. Yes, it is but a seeming absence of Intelligence, Mind, knowing and aware of being that which Mind really is.

That which seems to be invisible here really is Substance, Form, and Activity. And this Activity really is Mind, Intelligence, actively knowing—being actively aware of being just what Intelligence knows Itself to be. This really is all Substance in Form, and it is *this* Substance being Omniaction, all Activity, all that is active.

When knowledge, or conscious awareness of being complete, is complete, that which *appears* to be invisible really is visible. It is fully evident as the only Substance, Form, and Activity that is visible, right here, right now, and there is no awareness of solid, dark, dense matter to be visible. Thus, there is no matter.

Chapter X

God Is Light

God is Light. God is complete; thus, God is Completeness. This being true, it follows that Light is complete, total, entire. So there really is no darkness; thus, there is no darkness to transcend. All is Light, and there is no Substance in Form that is not Light.

Furthermore, there is no activity that is not Light in action. Anyone who experiences that aspect of illumination which reveals All to be Light is aware that this is a Universe that consists of Light. He is also aware that no darkness exists in, or as, this boundless Infinity which we call the Universe. We have stated before that Dr. Einstein spoke of Light as being a universal Constant. God is the ever complete Light that is a universal Constant. Thus, Light is not something that fluctuates. Neither is It something that comes and goes. Rather, Light is omnipresent; It is steady; It is omniactive; It is infinite, and It is eternal. This is Absolute Truth.

What is this omnipresent Light that is constant, infinite, and eternal? Beloved, the Light is conscious, living, loving Mind, Intelligence. It is the Intelligence that is all knowledge. It is interesting to note that frequently some Absolute Truth will be voiced by someone who has never studied or even read anything about the Absolute Truth Itself. For instance, we may hear someone say, "The light dawned," merely meaning that he knows something that he did not know before. Or again, he may say, "Oh, now I see the light," which, of course, is but another way of saying the same thing.

Light is the complete Intelligence that is all knowledge. How wonderful it is to know that Light is the universal Constant that is omnipresent, and this omnipresent Light is *all knowledge, all that is, or can be, known.*

Our Bible refers to Light in many aspects of Itself. Yet every aspect of the Light is the full and complete Light. In John 1:4, we read, "In him was life; and the life was the light of men." Here John speaks of the fact that Life is Light and that Light is Life. Furthermore, he clearly states that this Light is the very Life that is alive as Man. Then he reinforces this startling statement; he states: "That was the true Light, which lighteth every man that cometh into the world" (John 1:9).

Now, we are alive. Even though it *seems* that we came into the world, or were born, we really are and remain that Light. Otherwise, we could not be alive. So this Light that is Life is alive. Yes, It is an eternal, constant, living Substance in Form.

Now, we have the infinite universal Light presented as Mind (Intelligence) and Life; this means that the Universe consists of living Intelligence, or intelligent Life. But as we know, Intelligence, Life, and Consciousness are One. Again and again, we have said that Consciousness is Substance. Well, we are conscious of being alive; we are conscious of being Life. In fact, *we* are the Life that is conscious of being alive. Thus, the living Substance — Consciousness — that is alive as our Substance is the universal, ever-present Light.

Beloved One, just consider the tremendous spiritual significance of this Absolute Truth. Here it is clear that the Light that is alive right here and now, as this living, conscious Substance, is the constant Light that we see, and know to be, our own Being, or Life. We are absolutely sure of this fact when we, in illumination, see this entire Universe that consists of Light. Thus, Man, the uncreated, eternal Man — who is the Christ-Light — is the very Substance that is this Universe. It is not surprising that Jesus could say, "Ye are the light of the world" (Matt. 5:14). Yes, the ever-living Christ-Man *is* the conscious Life, the Light that lighteth the entire world. And this Light is even the Substance that *is* this entire Universe.

So often we have said, "This Universe is God, and God *is* this Universe." Well, in 1 John 1:5, we read, "God is light, and in him is no darkness at all." The God that is Light is the Light that is God. Knowing that God *is* this Universe, we also know that the very Substance, Form, and Activity which is this Universe is Light. Knowing that in, and *as*, God — the Light — there is no darkness at all, we also know that in, and as, this Universe there is no darkness.

There is no incomplete Mind (Intelligence). There is no deluded Consciousness. There is only Light, and Beloved, this Light is what we are.

Complete, conscious, living Intelligence is also Love. Light *is* Love. Without Love, there could be no Light, and without Light, there could be no Love. This is the entirety of the Substance, Form, and Activity that is the Universe. But this intelligent, conscious, loving Life that is alive right here and now is the entirety of your Substance, Form, and Activity. You could not be alive unless you were Light. You could not be conscious that you exist, unless you were the Light. You could not be intelligent at all, if you were not the Light. And you could not be loving at all, unless you were the Light that is Love.

Beloved, never yearn or long to be that which you already are. Never believe that you are not illumined. Never believe that you are not the Light that is infinite Life, the Life that is universal Life. Never make the mistake of imagining that someone is any more illumined than are you. Never make the mistake of wishing that you were as illumined, or enlightened, as anyone who exists. To do this is to deny your own ever-present enlightenment.

Regardless of any seeming failure to see the Light that *is*, just go right on, knowing full well that you are the full Light that lighteth *every* Man. When the complete evidence of being this Light is evidenced, you will realize that always you have been this Light and always you will be and remain this Light. This revelation, and the evidence of the revelation, comes when you least expect it. Never does this glorious Light fully reveal and evidence Itself when you are being troubled or anxious about it. Neither does It evidence Itself if you are dwelling on It or trying to compel this experience of illumination to be evident. It just doesn't happen.

Just go right on knowing that despite any appearance of darkness, or even partial darkness, you really *are* the "Light that shineth" right where the darkness seems to be. Furthermore, you are the Light in which there is no darkness at all. Never deceive your Self. Never limit your Self by imagining that you are any less the Light than is "every man that cometh into the world" of apparent darkness.

It is true that when you, in illumination, see the Universe of Light, you are seeing the Substance that is the Body of Light. But you also see that the Body of Light is not separate from, or other than, the infinite Light that is the Universe. And it is absolutely true that when you see the Body of Light, you are seeing the Substance—Light—that is this Universe. And again, you are aware that the Universe and the Body are one indivisible Substance. It *is* Light, and in and as this Light there is no darkness at all.

Then you really rejoice. It is pure ecstasy. Indeed, it is the *I Am that you are*. But always remember:

It is the I AM that you are right now, that you have always been and will always be. It is the I AM being the eternal Constant that is the full and complete Light.

Chapter XI

The Infinite Fulfillment of Purpose

God, the Universal All, fulfills His purpose by being All. This means that the fulfillment of God's purpose is in God being all Substance, all Form, and all Activity. Yes, God's infinite purpose is fulfilled by the Fact that God is the *only* Substance in action as everything and everyone. No one but God fulfills *any* purpose. There is no one other than God. Thus, there is no one but God who actually has any purpose to fulfill. The fulfillment of all purpose is infinite because Infinitude — God — is the purpose as well as being the fulfillment of the purpose.

Yet assumptive little supposedly born man, with breath in his nostrils and for whom there is no way to account, appears to have his own little selfish, separate purposes to fulfill. Furthermore, this same pseudo man imagines that the purpose to be fulfilled is his purpose and that he is the person that has to scheme, struggle, etc., in order to fulfill some selfish purpose. This completely fallacious illusion would — if it were possible — act as a resistance to God, the All, the Only, in the infinite fulfillment of His perfect purpose.

Assumptive man falsely believes that he can fulfill his separate, selfish purpose by thinking, scheming, plotting, planning, or doing. But God's infinite purpose is already constantly being fulfilled. This infinite, constant, omnipotent fulfillment is always going on because it is God in action, just being what God is, all that God is, and *only* what God is.

In our Bible, God is reported as asserting His infinite, indivisible fulfillment:

> Yea, before the day was I am he; and there is none that can deliver out of my hand: I will work, and who shall let it? (Isa. 43:13).

When the genuine, absolute significance of the foregoing statements is perceived, it is realized that they reveal a tremendously important, basic Truth. First, we have the Infinite All—God—announcing His Eternality. "Before the day was" denotes that even though infinite Intelligence—the complete Light—may not have been completely perceived, God, the infinite Light—Life—was alive as the Life, Intelligence, Consciousness, Love that exists as everyone and everything.

"And there is none that can deliver out of my hand" reveals the inseparability of the Infinite All One, God. Here is stated the irrevocable fact that there is nothing that can separate the indivisible Oneness that is God into something called God *and* man. Indeed, there is no separate born man. Yet there is God being the Christ—Man. But there is also the Christ—Man—being God. How, then, could there be such a thing as God *and* man? How could there be such a thing as man *and* God?

In the statement "I shall work, and who shall let it?" God is revealing the Absolute Ultimate Truth that He alone is the fulfillment of every purpose. The word *work* denotes activity. And of course, God *is* constantly in action. All Action is for the fulfillment of some purpose. But all action is Omniaction, or God being active. This means that the infinite Omni-action, which is God, fulfills His infinite purpose as all Activity, as all Substance and Form, being per-fectly active.

Beloved, the foregoing revelatory words concern-ing this verse from Isaiah present only a minimum of the many Truths revealed in these words. As you contemplate in full open Consciousness, many more Absolute Truths, behind and beyond the foregoing revelations, will be revealed as your own Con-sciousness.

In view of that which we have just perceived pertaining to Infinitude and Its infinite fulfillment of purpose, we might question, "Who or what exists that can oppose God in action? What could possibly act as a little pseudo-separate man that could inter-fere in any way with the omniactive fulfillment of purpose which is God, the indivisible All, in action?" We know that any resistance or opposition to the Universal All is utterly impossible.

The Bible also reports that God stated:

> For as the rain cometh down, and the snow
> from heaven, and returneth not thither, but
> watereth the earth, and maketh it bring forth and
> bud, that it may give seed to the sower, and
> bread to the eater: So shall my word be that goeth
> forth from my mouth: it shall not return unto me
> void, but it shall accomplish that which I please,
> and it shall prosper in the thing whereto I sent
> it (Isa. 55: 10, 11).

Oh, there are so many basic Absolute Truths
revealed in the foregoing quotations. But the full
open Consciousness that you are will experience the
revelation of these Absolute Truths.

You will not *try* to understand the words quoted
from our beloved Bible. Neither will you make any
effort to interpret them. Rather, you will simply read
them without any mental effort, perceive that Self-
revelation will fully reveal these Absolute Truths.
Nonetheless, it is very clear right now that these
quotations do reveal that God—Omniaction—is ever
the fulfillment of His purpose in being and that this
fulfillment of purpose is *always* successful. This fulfillment of purpose goes right on, despite the so-
called plotting, reasoning, etc., of any assumptive
born man.

It is impossible that this totally non-existent
appearance called born man could do anything of
himself. Least of all could he—even if he existed—
oppose Infinitude and fulfill some selfish, humanly
ambitious purpose. In our Bible, there are some
examples of the futility of all this plotting, scheming,

planning, doing, etc. For instance, let us consider the following quotations:

> I builded me houses, I planted me vineyards ... I gathered also silver and gold ... and the peculiar treasure of kings and of the provinces: So I was great and increased more than all that were before me in Jerusalem ... Then I looked on all the works that my hands had wrought, and on the labor that I had labored to do: and, behold, all was vanity and vexation of spirit, and there was no profit under the sun ... Then I saw that wisdom excelleth folly, as far as light excelleth darkness (Eccles. 2:4,8,9,11,13).

The foregoing quotations speak for themselves to those who really understand their genuine significance.

Jesus knew the futility of the scheming, plotting, planning of assumptive man with breath in his nostrils:

> And he spake a parable unto them, saying, The ground of a certain rich man brought forth plentifully; and he thought within himself, saying, What shall I do, because I have no room where to bestow my fruits?

> And he said, This will I do: I will pull down my barns, and build greater; there will I bestow all my fruits and my goods. And I will say to my soul, Soul, thou hast much goods laid up for many years; take thine ease, eat, drink, and be merry.

> But God said unto him, Thou fool, this night thy soul shall be required of thee: then whose

shall those things be, which thou hast provided?" (Luke 12:16-20).

It is truly wonderful to realize that every Absolute Truth we can ever perceive or know can be found right here within the pages of our beloved Bible. As we have stated in earlier writings, we do not mean that it is wrong to be actively fulfilling our purpose in being. It is not wrong to live comfortably, beautifully, with an abundance of supply. But what Jesus does reveal in this parable is the futility of the plotting, planning, scheming, struggling, thinking, etc., of this little assumptive man with breath in his nostrils.

He makes this very clear, when, immediately following the foregoing parable, he continues:

> Take no thought for your life ... And seek not ye what ye shall eat, or what ye shall drink, neither be ye of doubtful mind. For all these things do the nations of the world seek after: and your Father knoweth that ye have need of these things. But rather seek ye the kingdom of God; and all these things shall be added unto you. Fear not, little flock; for it is your Father's good pleasure to give you the kingdom (Luke 12: 22, 29-32).

We know that *kingdom* means Consciousness. To seek the kingdom of God means to be full open Consciousness, in order that the God-Consciousness—which we are—may perceive that all you can ever seek, or seek to be, you already constantly, eternally are.

Oh, there are so many Absolute Truths that are revealed in just the foregoing parable and the sayings of Jesus that follow it. I hope you will contemplate much, as full open Consciousness, on the above mentioned parable and also on the sayings of Jesus right after the parable was revealed. You will be delighted with the revelations. It is helpful to study and contemplate all of the parables of Jesus. There is far more Absolute Truth to be perceived between and beyond the lines than is generally realized. I marvel at the great wealth and depth of the Absolute Truth revealed in these parables.

But now, let us pursue our subject of the infinite fulfillment of purpose and the fact that this infinite fulfillment of purpose can, and does, go on without thinking, scheming, plotting, or planning—and above all, without the seeming effort of assumptive man.

On page three in *The Gospel According to Thomas,* we find Jesus speaking of that which is necessary to complete Self-discovery and Self-revelation. But here we also find that which we can expect to experience once our genuine and *only* God I AM is revealed. He frankly states that, for awhile, we may seem to be troubled. But then he makes it very clear that following this seeming disturbance we will marvel and that we will discover the Omnipotence that is God to be the Love that is Power.

Furthermore, in his statements it is obvious that we are to perceive that the God I AM is the *I* that we are, and the I AM that we are is Omnipotence—God

Himself. But this Power that is Love is not power to influence, to dominate, or to rule over anyone or anything. Even though Jesus speaks as though we would "reign" or have dominion over all, he does not mean that we are to have power over anyone called "another." Rather, it is that Jesus refers to our complete revelation that *this right here is the Kingdom of God*. We are in the Kingdom—Consciousness—that is God, and we *are* the Kingdom—Consciousness— that is God.

The Kingdom and the King are one and the same. The King—Consciousness—that is Self-revealed and the Kingdom—Consciousness—of being just what God *is* are one and the same enlightened Consciousness. Therefore, we stand in the face of anything and everything that would seem to present a picture of darkness, trouble, inharmony, etc., and we *stand*, fully aware of being the Presence of the Power and the Power of the Presence.

Oh yes, we do seem to sincerely seek and seek. When we truly find that which we have apparently been seeking, we discover that it has not really been a search at all. Rather, all the while, it has been that which is *found*—the infinite *I* that I am, signifying, and even asserting, Its Presence. Then when we seem to be troubled—no matter how terrible or convincing any appearance may *seem* to be—we just don't believe it. We know, and we see things as they *are*. We are totally unconcerned about anything that is merely an appearance. Furthermore, we know that even the appearance signifies the omnipotent Omnipresence which is God, hence, the absolute, untroubled, perfect God I AM that we are. Then, beloved One, we reach the glorious point of no return, and here there can never be any turning back. We can never even *seem* to see or to experience trouble, illness, problems, or inharmony of any kind. Here we stand as the universal, eternal Constant which is *Light Itself*.

So now we realize that, being conscious only as the God-Consciousness, we are already aware of being the fulfillment of our purpose in being. We also realize that it is Infinitude fulfilling Its purpose in being by being what we are, all that we are, and only that which we are and have been forever. Here we make no effort to *do* something of and as any little assumptive self. We do not try to know something through thinking, reasoning, or any mental gymnastics. Above all, we do not try to be something. We know that we could not be anything at all, if we were not the boundless, eternal, constant, Infinite All, just being.

> We truly *know* that we only exist as the infinite fulfillment of purpose, fulfilling Its purpose by being the God I AM that we eternally are.

Chapter XII

The Eternal, Immutable, Constant Substance that Is

It is exceedingly important that we truly know —and *know* that we know—the genuine Nature of Substance. Yes, we must see, know, and experience being the absolute, perfect, eternal, constant, immutable Substance that we actually *are*.

In order to know, thus see and be, the true and *only* Substance that exists, we must perceive the Absolute Ultimate that all Substance is Consciousness. Consciousness is all Substance. All Substance is an eternal, immutable, *living* Substance. All that is alive is Substance. All living Substance is in Form, and all Substance is active. Actually, all Substance *is* the immutable, omniactive Omniaction, surging and flowing as innumerable rhythmic tempos. But *all of this is Consciousness in action*.

It is also important that we perceive the Absolute Truth that our own awareness—Consciousness— that we exist is the Substance that exists as every Form and as every rhythmic tempo that is active as this Substance in Form. It is impossible to stress too decidedly the fact that our very omniactive Consciousness that we exist is our Substance. It is the Substance that is the tree, the bird, the planet, the star, and even every stone or pebble. Oh yes, *our Consciousness that we exist is our Substance, our Form, and our Activity*. You see, Consciousness *is* the Substance, even as Substance is Consciousness.

We—Consciousness, Life, Mind, Love—are all one and the same. Thus, all Substance is Life, Love, Mind (Intelligence) Consciousness. Consciousness is Infinitude, God. God—Infinitude—is the only Substance. Infinite, omnipresent, omniactive Substance is eternal. This eternal Substance is indestructible, imperishable, and immutable. How could it be possible for God, the only Substance, to exist as a kind of substance that could be or become imperfect? How could the Substance that is God perish or be destroyed? How could the immutable, ever-perfect Substance, Consciousness, that is God ever change from Perfection into imperfection? It couldn't, and it doesn't.

Nothing can happen, nothing can go on, in and as *any* Substance that is not happening, is not going on, in and as the Substance—Consciousness—that is God. Since God, the only Substance, *is* eternal Life, what substance exists that can die, or cease to exist? Life exists and is alive eternally. Since God—the *only* Substance—is constant, immutable Absolute Perfection, what substance exists that can be temporary, mutable, or imperfect? Since there is Substance in Form here called a Body, whose Substance in Form *is* this Body? Does it not have to be the Substance that is God in Form? Indeed so. Then is it not the very Body of God, or God's Body? There really is one Body and one Spirit — Consciousness — which are God's.

Yes, there really is but one Substance *being* a Body. There really is but one Spirit, or Consciousness, that is aware of being the Body. God, aware of being the Body, *is* the Body. Actually, God, the only Consciousness — Substance — aware of being the Body is all that exists right here and now as the Body. And God, Omniaction, actively conscious of being the Body, is the *only* activity going on in, or as, the bodily activity right here and now.

Beloved, Infinity is conscious because Infinity is Consciousness. It is conscious of Being and of being just what It is. Infinity is God, this boundless Universe. This Universe is conscious because It consists of Consciousness. Consciousness is the Substance that *is* this Universe. This is a conscious Universe. It is alive. It is a boundless, living Substance, and It is conscious of being just what It is.

Yes, this Universe is alive, and It is *consciously* alive as the omnipresent, living Substance that is indivisibly all Substance — Consciousness — in Form. This is an intelligent Universe. It consists of living, intelligent Consciousness.Its Substance is intelligent, livi ng Consciousness. But above all, this Universe is a loving Universe. It consciously loves. It intelligently loves. It consists of intelligent, omniactive Love. Its Substance is intelligent, living, loving Consciousness.

In orthodoxy, sometimes we would almost desperately cry out, "Oh, God, do you hear my prayer?" And sometimes in moments of great seeming trouble, we felt that there was no God around who knew anything about us. Even after we began the study of metaphysics, sometimes we would ask whether or nor God knew anything about our pain, our trouble, or despair. But this hopelessness and doubt could only seem to be because we evidently were not aware of the glorious fact that God—Consciousness—is the Substance that is totally complete and equally omnipresent as every one of us. To know that this is a living, loving, intelligent, conscious Universe is really to know about what God is and thus to *know* God.

It is wonderful to know that the Consciousness that is our Substance *is* this conscious Universe being conscious—yes, consciously being our Substance. But it is equally wonderful to know that our Substance is conscious of being the Substance that is this Universe.

Sometimes someone will object to this Absolute Truth and say, "But I can't see Consciousness. I can't hear Consciousness. I can't feel Consciousness. I can't touch Consciousness." Oh yes, you *can* see and hear Consciousness. You can see the Substance that is Consciousness whenever you actually see the Body or any Substance in Form. You can hear Consciousness whenever you actually hear the glorious Voice of Consciousness. It matters not whether this Voice is heard in song or speaking as the very Love that is God—Consciousness—Itself. You do hear Consciousness.

You *can* touch Consciousness. Whenever you lovingly caress someone or just compassionately touch his or her hand, you have touched Love, which is Consciousness. This does not mean that you have seen, heard, or touched any Consciousness that is separate from, or other than, the Consciousness that you are.

Above all, you can *feel* Consciousness. You know the feeling when warm, liquid Love surges and flows in and as the Consciousness that you are. This Love is a living, conscious experience, and *It is Substance.*

Sometimes this Substance in Form—Consciousness—is called the Body of Light. And it is indeed Light. There really is a Body of Light, and It is alive, It is intelligent, It is loving, and It is conscious. Indeed, It *is* Consciousness. And this Body of Light *can* be seen. It is visible. It is being seen clearly and definitely. Sometimes it seems that It shines right through the seeming darkness that apparently is superimposed over this Body of Light. However, generally, this Body of living Light is all that is seen as the Body, and the seemingly superimposed darkness is completely obliterated.

Nonetheless, this Body of Light is actually Substance in Form. It is this Body that walks, moves, and acts here, and no other. It is this Body of Light that is alive, intelligent, and loving right here. But don't be deceived; rightly seen, even the seeming superimposed body itself, is not something else, or other, than the Body of Light. It truly is the Body of Light—Consciousness—but It is being seen incompletely, or mistakenly.

It is not the body that is apparent darkness that appears to cover the Body of Light. Rather, it seems to be our ignorant or imperfect way of seeing this truly visible Body that makes it *appear* to be solid, dark, and dense. Yet as we know, there is only *one* Substance, and this Substance is Consciousness. Therefore, even that which is misinterpreted to be solidity, density, darkness, really is this one indivisible Consciousness in Form.

Now, there is one more point that must be perceived since we are to clearly realize just what this Body really is. Since no one has two bodies, we are speaking of the one and only Body, whether it appears to be solidity, density, etc., in Form or whether it is seen as the Body of ever-living Consciousness which is Light.

All of us know that the physcists state that the nucleus at the center of the atom is light, and this light is called energy. Now, Energy is Life, even as Light is Life. There is not one separate nucleus. But the innumerable, indivisible nuclei that comprise this Body are omniactive Light, Life, Intelligence, Love.

Beloved, this Substance that is this Body right here—whether we see It as Light or whether we see It as something that appears to have weight, that appears to be solid, dense or dark — it makes no difference; *it is all the same Substance*. In the Psalms we find David singing, "The darkness and the light are both alike to thee." And this fact is assuredly true pertaining to this Body right here.

Many of the Buddhistic faith feel that we must rid ourselves of this Body that appears to be dark and solid before we can perceive the Body of Light or experience being this Body of Light. This simply is not true. We must transcend that which is called death, and this awareness is beginning to take place. We are to know that this Body is eternal, even as this Identity is eternal. Therefore, this Body is not to be destroyed or to perish.

The Bible says that God "hath no pleasure in the death of him who dieth (Ezek. 18:32). Also, it says that "death is swallowed up in victory" (1 Cor. 15:54). And again we read, "the last enemy that shall be destroyed is death" (1 Cor. 15:26). Well, isn't it the Body that is supposed to die? That cruel deception which is called death will never be transcended until we accept the Absolute Truth that the Body that seems to be born, that *appears* to be temporary, and the Body that is known to be Light, Consciousness, Life Itself, are one indivisible Body. This one everlasting Body may be seen either as enlightened Consciousness or as a seeming incomplete awareness. However, no matter how it may appear, the actual and only Body, consisting of Consciousness, Light (Life), and Mind (Intelligence) is, and remains, forever the same. Actually, that which seems to be a body of darkness, weight, solidity, really is the Body of Light Itself. And of course, this Body of Light consists of *living* Consciousness, *living* Intelligence, and *living* Love.

It is all a matter of just how this one indivisible Body is seen. For instance, the Grand Canyon, viewed from the standpoint of one who still seems to be buried in seeming materialism, can appear to be one essence and form. But to the one who is aware of the Fact that all Substance is Consciousness, Light, it can be seen as that which it actually *is*. To the scientific so-called mind, it can be analyzed from that particular standpoint. But to the truly enlightened Consciousness, it can be — and is — seen to be eternal, changeless grandeur, Beauty, Art, Music, and All that Consciousness actually *is*.

Beloved, this is not duality. We do not intend to convey the impression that there are two Consciousnesses or two Visions. Of course, it is impossible to really see anything that does not exist at all. So it is not a matter of "twoness" or "otherness." Rather, it is all a matter of seeing with, and *as*, the Vision Infinite but *seeming* to see merely an appearance of that which genuinely does exist.

The physicists know that Substance is not at all the way it appears to be. They are not deceived by an appearance of solidity, etc. Well, then, knowing the true Nature of Substance and Activity, surely it is not necessary for us to be misled by an appearance. As stated before, an appearance is merely an appearance, and it actually is not at all the Substance that *is*. Yet no matter how it seems to be seen, it remains the very same glorious, limitless, beginningless, changeless, endless Consciousness. This is Love in action. It can be—and is—seen, no matter whether the one who sees it is fully aware of being the Light or not. This, dear One, is Love and Love in action.

In like manner, this Body or any Substance in Form can be viewed by anyone who is supposedly merely intellectual, and it will seem to consist of born substance in form, a substance that is temporary and subject to all the so-called laws of temporary, assumptive born man. But to the Consciousness that is Light Itself, this Substance reveals Itself to be the eternal, birthless, deathless Substance—Consciousness—which is Light Itself. Yet it is the same Substance in Form. It is the very same Body. And it matters not at all how It is seen. The Consciousness that is this Body knows only that which It is, and It is entirely unconcerned as to how It is being seen or viewed. Nothing changes the Substance and Activity that really are the eternal Body that consists of Consciousness—Light—Motion, Activity.

Beloved, it is well to realize that there can be no duality in our perception of Substance in Form, whether it be called tree, dog, flower, bird, or the Body that is called Man. It is all the one indivisible Substance.

Now, we know the Nature of this Substance. What is necessary is to be equally aware of this Substance in Form *evidenced*. So often it seems we consider the evidence of Absolute Perfection as something to be hoped for tomorrow or perhaps next year. Right here, it would appear that we are being dual.

> The evidence of Absolute Perfection is not something that is separate from the Substance that is evidenced.

There is no such thing as omniactive Substance in Form *and* the evidence that is this Substance in Form, constantly, eternally.

To consider the evidence of Absolute Perfection in Form and the absolute, perfect Substance in Form as though they were two, rather than one integral One, is duality. Actually, the Body of everything you see *is* Light. For instance, the trees, the flowers, the grass, even the pavement, the car, etc., *consist of Light*, and this Light is the only Substance that is evidenced right here. This is identically the same Light that we often see as the Substance that is this Body. But it is well to perceive that this Light is the genuine and only Substance being perfectly and rightly seen. Nonetheless, although that which is right within your view may seem to be solid, dark, and dense, if that which you are viewing were not actually that specific Substance in Form, there could be no seeming image of darkness, density, solidity.

So the evidence is right within your view. This is the evidence. In fact, *you* are the evidence of things apparently unseen.

Chapter XIII

God Alone Is Power

Only that which God *is*, and knows Himself to be, has validity or is valid. Only that which God is, and *knows* Himself to be, is Power. Only that which God is aware of being is true, valid, and omnipotent. Only when God says I AM can that statement really be made. Only when God says I AM can that statement be true. God alone can say I AM *THAT* I AM. The omnipotent statement of Being is I AM THAT I AM.

This wonderful statement means that we can joyously say, and in this way *only* can we say:

> I am the evidence of the fact that God *is*. I am the evidence of the Presence of God—of God being present—right here and right now. I cannot be the evidence of anything that is not God, for there is nothing but God to be evidenced.

Who or what exists that can stop or interfere with God being the evidence of what God *is*? I could not compel myself to be God's evidence of Himself. Neither can I compel myself to be God's evidence of what God is not. I have no choice; I have to be the I AM that is God evidencing Himself. There can be no evidence that is not omnipotent Omnipresence evidencing Itself.

Therefore, the necessity is always to see as God sees, perceive as God perceives, and to be aware as God is aware. This means to keep the Mind stayed on God, as our Bible states. Yes, we must keep the Mind that we *are* constantly aware of being just what God *is* and constantly perceive as the intelligent Consciousness that is God perceiving. Therefore, we do not permit supposedly born mind to recognize, honor, or consider the things of the world. In this way only can we be aware *as* Perfection being perfect; eternal Life being eternally alive; Wholeness, Completeness, being constantly and eternally whole, complete Absolute Perfection. Only in this way can we consciously evidence this beautiful Absolute Truth that we know and that we are.

We are not concerned with people as such, or per se. We do not consider any assumptive born man. But we do consider God, who is aware of *being* that one, that tree, that bird, or whatever. No matter what the given name of anyone—Mary, John, or whatever—that one is God, aware of being *that one*. Yet it is still God aware of being God.

That which is called a given name is just that. It is merely a name that is given to a supposedly born man. Nonetheless, it does denote the Presence of just what God is, and is aware of being, as that specific Identity, or identification of Himself. But this is not all. No matter what the given name may be, *that One—that Identity—is God*, aware of being just what

God is and aware of being All that God is, as *that* one.

There are some who object to the constant repetition ef the word *God* in the Ultimate. Of course, this wonderful word may seem repetitive, and this is particularly true if one does not *experience* that glorious surge of Love, of warmth, of living Light as the word *God* is uttered or considered. I *love* this word. It is impossible to describe the feeling of awe, yet of power, of humility, of joy, serenity that is experienced when this word is even whispered. Often, so very often, I am impelled to cease some activity of the moment and just softly whisper over and over again the beautiful word, *God, God, God.*

There could not possibly be any ego in this experience. There are those who often say that they can understand this Absolute Truth intellectually, but they cannot feel the Light, the Love, the Allness, and Onliness that is this God-Presence. Please be assured that just to be full open Consciousness and to utter this word—so fraught with power, Love, tenderness—does reveal the wonderful fact that *you cannot, never have, and never could understand or feel this word intellectually.* The so-called intellect—if such existed—would supposedly be centered in an assumed born brain. There *is* no such thing as a born body, so how could there be a born brain? So, beloved One, you can rejoice that you recognize, accept, and love God—this Absolute Truth. Never rob your Self of the sheer joy, the ecstasy, of God Self-perception and revelation by claiming that you can only understand God intellectually.

In the Consciousness of the Identity that I am, there are two words of paramount importance. Yet these two words are really but one. Always, when I speak, write, or hear the word *God*, the word *Love* is simultaneously heard and felt. In like manner, when I utter, hear, or feel the Presence that is Love, the word *God* is felt. Of course, constantly there is that awareness that the word *God* really means All, Everything, omnipresent Infinity, and all that could possibly exist. But somehow the words *God* and/or *Love* are particularly and more frequently in my Heart.

Now, someone may say, "Oh, this is beautiful, but it is too vague. It doesn't give me anything definite to work with." Beloved One, I have seen and experienced that which the world calls miracles as the words *God* or *Love* were being uttered and felt. So there is Power in action specifically—and of course, infinitely—whenever these two words are uttered and felt. So this God who is Love and the Love that is God is indeed practical, irresistible, omnipotent Presence.

Perhaps it may seem that you are experiencing some aspect of imperfection. In this instance, you would consider, first of all, God—the All—and as full open Consciousness, feel this gentle, loving, ever-flowing Allness actually being the Entirety of your Substance, Form, and Activity. Often the appearance of imperfection simply disappears in just such an experience as has been mentioned. Then it may happen that the word *Perfection* will literally flood your Consciousness. And of course, you know — without any thought-taking or effort of any kind — that God is omnipresent Absolute Perfection. You cannot compel yourself to know these Truths. Rather, it is that suddenly you are aware of the Presence that is God, being Absolute Perfection.

Furthermore, you are conscious of *being* the specific Absolute Truth you have been perceiving. It is all Self-revelation, and you will clearly perceive that you *are* that infinite, indivisible, omnipresent Absolute Perfection which is God being perfect. Yes, no doubt you will realize that your awareness of being Absolute Perfection is God, conscious of being constantly, eternally perfect.

Now, again it must be mentioned that during this beautiful experience, you have not engaged in any meditation; you have certainly not concentrated on the word *Perfection*, and neither have you gone through any thought processes. It is just as though you were listening to beautiful music or viewing a beautiful work of art. Actually, you realize that the Beauty of the music *is*, the beauty of the art *is*, and you are merely considering that perfect Beauty that *is*.

Well, Absolute Perfection *is*. And you find that you are just considering the Absolute Perfection which *is*. It is as simple as that. A child will instantly perceive this Truth. Actually, children often speak the Absolute Truth so spontaneously that we are surprised. Then sometimes some adult will falsely imagine that the child has been daydreaming. It is not surprising that Jesus stated, "A little child shall lead them." Oh, it is all so simple and so effortless. *And it is so practical.*

Then again, it might appear that Supply was inadequate or perhaps even missing from your experience. Should this be the case, the full open Consciousness you are will consider the boundless Completeness that is God. You may find that the word *Completeness* is present in and as the Consciousness that you are. Again, the absolute, indivisible Completeness which is Supply may surge and flow as your Consciousness of Being. During all this effortless consideration of the Supply that is, you have never once considered any such fallacy as limitation, lack, insufficiency, etc.

Beloved One, please realize that no matter what so-called inharmony or abnormalcy may *seem* to be presented, it is in this same glorious way that you will find Self-revelation evidencing Itself. You will realize that only that which eternally exists is, or can be, visibly evidenced and experienced. Above all, you will know that you have not done anything in order to make that which already *is* become that which it has always been, is now, and will always continue to be. No one can bring God into being. No one can make God be God. No one can force Absolute Perfection to become perfect. And no one can bring the infinite Supply that *is* into being or into becoming an eternal Constant.

Now, one may say, "But what about my activity? I can't see how this Absolute Truth can manifest Itself as the evidence of perfect Activity." Here again, you may "consider the heavens," as our Bible states. Consider the absolute, perfect, effortless activity of the stars, the planets, the galaxies, etc. Perhaps you will consider the fact that our Earth planet is not something that is separate from the heavens and that it is in constant, perfect, intelligent action eternally. It would never occur to you that the activity of this planet was labored, strained, or difficult. Neither would it occur to you that this perfect Activity could ever be resisted, restricted, or hindered in any way.

Then, perhaps, the words *infinite, intelligent Omniaction,* or any words which signify God, Infinity in action, will be surging and flowing as the Consciousness that you are. Of course, the word *Omniaction* means God in action to the Identity that I am. But this is true because God signifies *everything* and *everyone,* as far as I am concerned. At any rate, the Self-revelation of the infinite, indivisible, everywhere present, perfect, effortless Activity is the *only* Activity.

As this Absolute Truth reveals Itself as your Consciousness, you will find that It is manifesting Itself as your bodily activity. Surely the Omnipotence that manifests Itself as this entire, boundless Infinity in action is also the Power that manifests Itself as *this* perfect, effortless bodily activity. As stated so often: there is nothing about the delineation that is manifested as the form of your Body that interferes with the infinite, irresistible activity effortlessly functioning as this Body right here and now.

Oh, the seeming problems that may confront us may appear to be numerous and varied. Yet there can be no darkness so dense that the Light is ever completely obscured. There is absolutely nothing existing that can preempt the *one* and *only* Presence, God.

There are some points that must be clarified here, and then we will continue on to our next subject. First of all, you will realize that the Truths revealed here do not present a "method" or even a "way" for you to follow in your contemplation. You can only contemplate in the way that is revealed as *your* Consciousness. All that has been presented here is the way that the Consciousness that I am reveals Itself. You will never limit or rob your Self by following the way that is revealed to you by any Consciousness other than the I AM Consciousness that *you are.*

Now, let us consider this all-important word *God* for a moment. As stated before, this word signifies Love, even as Love signifies God in my experience. Thus, the word *Love* also signifies *everything* and *everyone.* Now, perhaps some other word rather than *God* may signify to you the same meaning that the word *God* means as my experience. But no matter what word or combination of words may signify God to you, if you do not feel and experience *being* this glorious, tender Love, it may very well seem that contemplation feels incomplete, and you will sometimes feel unsatisfied.

So beloved One, if the word *infinitude, ocean,* *pebble,* or whatever, brings a feeling of the boundless, All-Presence that is Love Itself, by all means, let the word that is *your* word reveal as it will. Of course, really, no words are actually necessary. In fact, the *Presence* is indescribable in words. This Presence is *always* surging and soaring as the Consciousness we are. It is only occasionally that we hear or utter the words. Generally we feel no necessity for words. But sometimes we hear or utter them just for the sheer joy of it.

One final statement that is of the utmost impor-tance:

Love is the Power of all our seeing. Love is the Power of all our Being. Let come whatever word that will, the Power is Love; all else is still but tinkling and sounding brass.

Chapter XIV

There Is No Becoming

Just recently, I received a splendid letter from a nuclear physicist. For quite a while he has been studying and contemplating the writings of the Ultimate. He states that from his education, experiments, and knowledge as a nuclear physicist, he knows that every word in the writings is absolutely true. (Incidentally, you may be interested to know that among those who are interested in the writings of the Ultimate, there are many who are engaged in the nuclear activity. Also, there are several who are astronomers and some astrophysicists, and they are in agreement on the rightness of the Absolute Truth revealed in these writings). But to continue: the writer of the letter mentioned above wrote: "The Absolute Truth enables one to discover himself." Then he joyously stated, "Farther than this you cannot go."

This is really true. You see, the Self completely revealed is the *complete* Self revealed, and the complete Self revealed is God completely revealed. It is true that we continue on as ever greater God-Self perception, but we no longer seek to learn more *about* God. We no longer seek to become more like God or more Godlike. Rather, we abide in, and as, the ever greater perception which is the Absolute God-Self completely aware of *being* the only Self. Therefore, we realize that never can we become the absolute, complete God-Self that we *are*. Never can there be an unfinished Kingdom, or Consciousness. All is eternally complete — constantly, infinitely, eternally. Truly, it is wonderful and glorious to realize that never were we actually a seeker. Now we are not seeking, and never will we seek to know more about the Entirety of our Consciousness. Now we *know*, and this is everlasting.

The generally accepted opinion by scientists and religionists is that man is constantly improving, growing more perfect and upright. But our Bible states that, "God hath made man upright; but they have sought out many inventions" (Eccles. 7:29). Most physicists believe that man is in a constant state of evolution, gradually evolving into a better state of being, both mentally and bodily. The religionists, for the most part, believe that man is growing more spiritual, more loving, etc. Actually, neither the physicists nor the religionists actually know the true Nature and Substance that is Man.

The metaphysicians believe that man must constantly put off, or overcome, the assumptive, mortal sense of being until he *becomes* immortal. Of course, the latter is a higher sense of that which is Man. But even the belief that man must gradually emerge from the mortal to the immortal is a misconception of the eternal, immutable, constant Nature of the *only* Man who does, or can, exist.

As so often stated, God being the Christ is Man. The Christ being God is Man. Man being the Christ is God being. Thus, God, the Christ, and Man are all One and the same Being. God being need not become better in order to be the absolute, eternal, constant Perfection that is God. No one could imagine the ever-present, immutable, pure Christ having to evolve into a better, or more perfect, Christ. Well, the Christ, God, and Man, being the same, it is not only unnecessary but it is impossible that Man could ever become any better than Man eternally, constantly is.

All that Man is ever going to be, he is right now. All that Man has ever been, he is right now. That which already constantly *is*, is never in a state of becoming. How can Man become that which Man already is? He can't and He doesn't. Can God become more upright, more finished, more complete than God is? Is it necessary for God to go through an evolutionary process in order for God to be All that God is? What is Man? Is Man something of himself, separate from, or other than, God, the All, being All? We know the answers to these questions.

Now, who is Man that he can go through a process of improvement? Is Man something of and by himself that he can perfect or improve? There simply is no such man. God, the Whole, the All, the Totality, Completeness—the All that is All—can never be any more, any less, or any other than the Completeness that is God. God could never limit Man. To do so would mean that God could limit the illimitable, boundless, All-powerful Self. It is true that assumptive man—if such there were—could appear to limit himself. But again, there is no such man.

Even many of us who consider ourselves to be Absolute seem to fall into this trap—namely, *the fallacy of becoming*. Some of us seem to mistakenly imagine that we must gradually become more enlightened. This is tantamount to saying, "I am only partially alive, partially conscious, partially intelligent and loving. But I must and will become more alive, more intelligent, and more loving." Oh, yes, it is telling your Self that you are not complete, that you are not completely conscious, not completely alive, not completely intelligent, not completely loving, but that if you try very hard, you will become complete. Of course, you will also imagine that this improvement will have to take place in something called time and that it will be a long, slow process. Not a very pleasant prospect, is it?

In a humorous and ridiculous way, this situation is reminiscent of the following story, which most of us have heard. You will recall the story of the farmer's horse who balked at pulling the heavily loaded wagon. But the farmer shrewdly fastened a contraption to the end of the branch of a tree. On the end of the branch, he tied a carrot so that it dangled directly in front of the horse but just out of reach. The poor horse really wanted that carrot, so he started to run; but no matter how fast he ran or how hard he stretched, strained, and tried, he just couldn't reach that carrot. For all we know, he may still be running.

Of course this is silly. But laughter is really God thoroughly enjoying Himself, so we do indulge in this spontaneous laughter. Seriously, however, there really is a fact that this story points up. The fact is that so long as we go on attempting to improve, to *become* more spiritual, more upright, more perfect, or whatever, we can never attain our goal. You see, always we seem to see it as something to be accomplished at some future time—when there is no time. It appears that we are blocking this goal from being manifested now by denying it to be already a present Truth, or Fact. In short, if we deny the Presence of that Completeness we are right now, we are also denying the evidence of this Presence.

Another way in which the foregoing story can be a simile is the fact that the harder we try to become the complete, absolute, pure, perfect Man— that we already are—the more dense will seem to be our unawareness of being that Christ-Man now.

Many of us seem to feel that we must gradually become more and more enlightened, until finally we become the Light Itself. Often this fallacy is engendered because we seem to have a tendency to imagine that someone is more enlightened than we are. Beloved, truly we are being unfair and unloving to our Christ-Self if we continue to deny being this complete Christ-Light.

There are also other aspects of this fallacy that should be considered. For instance, sometimes this mistaken sense of the complete Christ-Self will seem to bring about a false sense of discouragement. Often we will say, "Oh, I can never be as enlightened as Tom Smith or Jennie Jones. How can I ever hope to attain the great illumination that is realized and experienced by him — or her?" Then a false feeling of inferiority and discouragement seems to creep in. Sometimes there is an almost fatalistic hopelessness engendered by just imagining that somehow we were not meant to be the full, complete Light. This fatalistic attitude is terrible. It is almost as horrendous as is the theory that we have sinned in a previous life and must work out our karma. *There is no Love in this, and there can be no God in such a cruel misconception.*

There is just one more aspect of this self-deception that we shall consider. Despite the seeming dualistic terminology employed here, you realize that the one and only Man, who is the Christ-Consciousness, is never deceived. It is only the self-betrayal that is symbolized by Judas that makes it appear there is such a thing as a self-deceived man, with breath in his nostrils. Sometimes the feeling of being less the Light than is John or Jennie will bring on almost a frenzied burst of determination to become as enlightened as is anyone.

Then comes the struggle, the effort, the frustration engendered by seeming failure to attain the heights of the goal that is being sought. Oh, there is such a seemingly desperate feeling, as the sense of hurry and of so-called time passing, and still the light seems to elude us. Then too, there seems to be a great sense of strain and struggle, and we appear to become impatient with anything that seems to interfere with our so-called progress. Thus, it is apparent that to attempt to *become* the full, complete Light that we are is inadvisable, disappointing, and futile.

The paradoxical aspect of some who really do experience illumination is their seeming failure to realize it for what it is. There are so many who falsely imagine that the only illumination that can be complete is in seeing the Universe, or the Body, as Light. This simply is not the case. In our book, *You Are The Splendor*, many aspects of illumination are mentioned, and there are many more aspects of illumination that are not included in this book. It is a mistake to believe that the only complete illumination is experienced as Light. As we have mentioned earlier, illumination may be seen, heard, felt, or experienced in many ways where no visible Light is seen. Let us be through with this mistake of feeling frustrated because, at the moment, we do not experience illumination as Light. It is not that the visual Light is any more complete or greater than any aspect of illumination. It is only that we mention the Light more frequently.

Again and again, someone will say, "Oh, if I could only become enlightened enough to enable me to see the Universe and the Body as Light, I know I would experience the evidence of Perfection." Nothing could be further from the Truth. Actually, it is far more important for us to just realize—consciously *know*—that Light is God and God is All than it is to just drift around either trying to see the Light or seeing It and floating purposelessly along.

Whether or not we seem to see the Light, It *is*. Let us just accept this Absolute Fact in the same way that, although we do not ordinarily actually see God, we just know that God *is*. Sometimes we do not actually see the Light that is the sun, but we don't doubt for one moment that this Light *is*. Certain it is we don't struggle or strain in order to see the sun on a cloudy morning. We just go along, knowing that the sun really is here, that it is shining, and that presently we are going to see it again.

This same Truth is true where illumination as Light is concerned. Presently we *are* going to see the Light that *is*, so we don't struggle to become aware of this Light. No one makes an effort to try to see the sun through the clouds. We know it is unnecessary. In this same way, we do not make an effort to compel ourselves to become conscious of seeing and being this eternal, constant, glorious Light that *is*. But above all, let us not doubt the Presence of the Light. Neither will we doubt that we truly are this Light.

The Bible says, "Be ye not of doubtful mind." And in John 20:29, we find an example of how wonderful it is and how rewarding it is to just admit, acknowledge, and abide in and as the assurance that the Light *is* and that we *are* the Light Itself, even though we may not at the moment consciously see this Light to be the Universe or as the Light in Form that is this Body. When, after the resurrection, Jesus appeared in the room with the disciples, Thomas doubted very much that it could be Jesus. Then Jesus invited Thomas to examine the apparent nail wounds in his hands and his seemingly pierced side. This was enough to convince Thomas that what he considered to be the flesh and blood body of Jesus was really that same Jesus that he imagined he had seen crucified. Then "Jesus saith unto him, Thomas, because thou hast seen me thou hast believed; blessed are they that have not seen, and yet have believed."

Oh, there are so many Absolute Truths revealed in this episode in our Bible. It would be well to read and contemplate this particular verse quite often. But for now, let us not diverge from our specific point. We were discussing the fact that some of us seem to make the evidence of our conscious Perfection dependent upon our seeing the Universe and the Body as Light. Well, it is more important to just feel, with solid conviction, that God, the Universe, *is* Light, thus, the Body *is* Light, and let that glorious, positive sense of Being *be* the Christ-Light Consciousness that we are. Let us abide in, and *as*, this Consciousness, even though we may not seem to see, or experience, the evidence of this seeing and being the Absolute Truth at the moment.

We are never going to see, thus consciously be, the evidence of this constant, eternal, visible Body of Light by always postponing it. And we do seem to postpone it by the decision that we must delay this evidence by having to become it.

Let us accept, and abide in and *as*, the Absolute Truth. Let us accept the Fact that only God *is*, and God is Light. Therefore, this Body has to be Light. The Universe has to be Light. Abide in and as the Fact that only because God *is* can anything or anyone actually *be*—thus, we have to be the Light that is God. Otherwise, we would not be anything or anyone at all. There is *only one* Substance, Form, and Activity that we can possibly be because there is only one Substance, Form, and Activity that we *can* be. This Substance, Form, and Activity is the Light that comprises the complete, total Universe and the Body right here and now. We *are*—right now—the Light we seem to have been seeking.

It does appear that this deception of "becoming" is very tenacious and very subtle. This is not surprising when we consider the fact that throughout the ages assumptive man has been taught, and has believed, this fallacy. At any rate, we do appear to be deeply entrenched in this seeming apparent darkness. But be assured that it only requires a full open Consciousness for us to clearly perceive that which we constantly, eternally, and infinitely *are*.

This, Beloved, is another reason why being "full open" is so important. It is in this complete openness that we perceive and experience being the Completeness, the Eternality, and the Constancy that we eternally are. In and as full open Consciousness, we are fully aware of being just what God is, only that which God is, and All that God is.

When are we going to completely realize and evidence this Fact? Well, the very moment that we stop this fallacy of *any* separation from the Allness that is God being the Entirety that we are. Also, the revelation that because we are, this moment and eternally, *all* that God is completely dissolves any falsity that we can ever *become* the God being *I* that we already are. In and as this full open Consciousness, we clearly perceive that we are not attributes *of* God. Rather, we are aware that we consist of the very Life, Intelligence, Love, Consciousness which *is* God. At this point, we no longer even seem to postpone knowing what we are, being what we are, and above all, consciously aware of being all that we know God to be.

Yes, we are far more than just attributes of God. We actually are the entire Principle, God, Being. True it is that we are perfect. But we also are perfect only because we are the Principle—Perfection—Itself. We are eternal, but we are eternal only because we are the Principle—Eternality—Itself. We are alive, but we live only because we are the boundless Principle—Life—Itself. We are conscious, but we are conscious only because we are the Principle—Consciousness—Itself. We are loving, but we love only because we are the infinite, eternal, omnipotent, omnipresent Principle—Love—Itself. We are intelligent, but we are intelligent only because we are the very Principle, Intelligence—Mind—Itself. Whatever we are aware of being, we are aware of being the Principle which is the Essence and Activity that is That.

Only Completeness can be complete. Only Eternality can be eternal. Only Immutability can be immutable. In short, if there were such things as attributes of God—Principle—only the Principle Itself could be the Essence and Activity of Its own attributes. Beloved, the infinite Principle—God—exists, and It is all that does exist. God being *you* is the Principle existing *as* you. How, then, can you be a mere attribute of that which you are? Such a thing is impossible. Never can you be any more, or any less, of the Entirety that you *are*.

Every so-called instantaneous healing that has ever taken place has simply been the Principle—absolute, eternal, omnipresent Perfection—that *is* the Christ-Man, evidencing the Perfection that constantly *is* the Christ. Of course, you realize that we are still on that subject of "becoming." Principle never becomes. Principle is a universal, eternal Constant. We are the I AM Principle that *is*. Even as Principle is an eternal, universal Constant, so it is that we—the I AM that we are—are an eternal, universal Constant. Thus, we perceive that we, right here and now, are *being* all that we have ever been or can ever be.

Truly, there is no time. As we have often stated, there is no way in which we can measure time. Since All constantly and eternally *is*, how could it be possible to measure periods between events? It could not be, and it *isn't*. How, then, can there be such a thing as becoming? Once we perceive the Fact that the Fullness, the Completeness, is that which Man really *is*, we can never again be misled by the false theory of becoming. This Completeness—as stated before—is an eternal, constant, absolute Truth, or Fact. We also realize that *we are that Fact, or Truth*. It is in this perception that all fallacious limitations are transcended. They simply don't exist. All seeming boundaries of so-called time and space are obliterated. We literally soar, free, as the boundless, complete Freedom that we are. And our joy is indescribable.

Now, let us continue with our subject, "becoming." The world, as it appears to be, is considered in a hopeless situation. Many there are who are convinced that nuclear bombing will blow this planet right out of existence. Yet there are those who hope and believe that the world of assumptive man is becoming a better world or that men are emerging into better men. Be assured that assumptive man is never going to be any better or any better off than this suppositional man is right now. *There is no such man*. But the Truth eternally holds true of — and as — the Christ-Man that we are.

However, this authentic Man is the only Man that *is*, and it is because he is all that God is that he can never be any better or any better off than he is this moment. Man can no more emerge into a better man than God can emerge into a better God. This world does not have to become anything that it is not right now. Our world, right here and now, is just as complete, perfect, and entire as is the Presence of God, which it is. Beloved, this Earth is Heaven, no matter how impossible this Fact may seem to be at the moment.

Infinity, Here and Now

Oh, God, I would forever see,
the Heaven that must be
the All that is Infinity,
the All Thou art, Entirety.

Now, just a few more words on "becoming," and then we shall continue on to a new subject. As you know, often we seem to delay the manifestation of Absolute Perfection by feeling that we must become perfect. It is odd that we continue to accept this old empty theory, even though we now know better. Yet an awareness of the ever newness and ever nowness that we are precludes the possibility of our ever becoming any better or more perfect than we are right now.

> Where is the wise? Where is the scribe? Where
> is the disputer of this world? hath not God made
> foolish the wisdom of this world? (1 Cor. 1:20).

The intelligent All-Consciousness that is God does reveal the futility, the fallacy, of all so-called acquired knowledge. In just one flash of illumination, we may realize the seeming ignorance of all that has ever been learned or written pertaining to an imaginary world of assumptive born man. It makes no difference how long these so-called laws of nature, including born man, have been accepted and believed. Illumination reveals the total fallacy of accepting such supposed human conclusions. Indeed, God does reveal how foolish is the wisdom of this world as it appears to be.

Chapter XV

The Passover

To this day, the Passover is observed as a very special event to those of the Jewish faith. This event is observed in commemoration of the deliverance of the children of Israel from bondage to the Egyptians. What is the true significance behind and beyond the Passover? It signifies Man's transcendence from ignorance — darkness — to Knowledge, or Light.

Seeming ignorance, darkness, is slavery. Light, Knowledge, Enlightenment, is complete freedom. The so-called slavery pertains to supposedly born man. Freedom is the Light, which is the eternal Christ-Man, who is God manifested. But this is not all. The Passover also symbolizes the "passover" from duality to the Absolute — which, of course, means God is All, All is God. It would seem that the Israelites were loathe to leave the way of life with which they had become familiar and upon which they depended. In short, they were loathe to depart from their duality. Some of them even seemed to prefer their bondage to Egypt, in order that they might cling to their meager enticements and pleasures.

The children of Israel were not alone in this fallacy. This same situation signifies the duality that most of us seem to wish to continue to indulge.

Yes, even with all the hardships, the problems, the frustrations, and the heartbreaks, many of us are reluctant to leave Egypt. Are there not many of us who prefer to remain in bondage to the pleasures and the pains of so-called born man, with its darkness, ignorance, duality? And isn't this true because the world as it appears to be is familiar ground? Doesn't it seem that some of us are afraid to branch out into the seeming unknown country and to resolutely accept the Fact that God really *is* All—All really *is* God?

And some of us, even though we have started on our apparent journey from duality to the Absolute, do we not sometimes doubt the Absolute Power of this Truth? Do we not sometimes even resent the necessity to *abide* in, and as, the Absolute? Isn't it true that, just at first, we may seem to encounter our worst problems? Many of us have experienced the seeming fears and doubts of our early experience in and as the Absolute. Yet the way we *know*, and we continue on, knowing inherently that *this is the true way* that Jesus was speaking about when he said, "I am the way, the truth, and the life." And aren't we now so glad that we have continued on to the Light, which is Knowledge, the joy of knowing and knowing that we know? Indeed so.

We recall that when Moses returned from the mountain, he found the children of Israel worshiping idols which they had fashioned with their own hands. Doesn't this signify that they imagined it was necessary to have or to build something other than the All-Presence that is God, to which they might cling? And didn't they also imagine it was necessary to have something or some leader to revere and to worship? Our entire Bible, from the first chapter of Genesis through the final chapter of Revelation, signifies the so-called birth of man with breath in his nostrils, until in the last of the Book of Revelation it is revealed that God really is All—All really is God. This, Beloved, is the true meaning of the "city that lieth foursquare."

The record of Jesus, his words and works, signifies the record of each one of us who embarks upon the way of the Absolute. Of course, this is only a symbolic seeming, but it is true that once we are fully aware of the Allness, the Onliness, which is God, we do appear to face rejection. Our friends, yes, sometimes even our loved ones, turn away from us, even as the world of appearance rejects us. Yes, we can seem to be rejected and betrayed, even as that glorious Jesus appeared to be rejected and betrayed. It may seem sometimes that some of those whom we loved so much and so completely trusted appear to betray us through so-called selfishness, ambition, avariciousness, etc. Then we really do seem to suffer, even as Jesus appeared to suffer indignities, shame, and the cross. (Now, of course, we never forget that these doleful pictures are all—and only—the symbolic pictures *we* are painting.)

But finally, glory be, we do experience the resurrection which is the complete seeing and being that which God *is*, and nothing else. This, Beloved, is the glorious transcendence beyond the seeming. Now we are completely free from all duality, from all personality, all supposed separateness. Now we are free from all illusions of other persons who can reject or betray us. We now perceive that there really is One alone and there is not another. Now we know, and we know that we know, there are no "others." Therefore, there are no other persons who can possibly be anything or do anything. Oh, the freedom, the complete joy, of this knowing.

Now, in this portrayal of that which seemed to be Jesus' experience of rejection, betrayal, suffering, resurrection, we have the moving picture of that which seems to be our experience—from the so-called birth of man until the supposed birth is transcended in our awareness that we too, even as Jesus, are eternal, birthless, and deathless. This, Beloved, signifies *our* resurrection.

Did Jesus pity himself? We have no record that he indulged in self-pity. Even in the Garden of Gethsemene, when the disciples could not remain awake even for one hour, his only comment was, "Could ye not stay awake with me one hour?" Right here is where Jesus completely and fully perceived that God was—and is—his Entirety. And he knew that he had to be just what God is, for there was nothing other than God for him to be. He completely transcended all false personal sense. In short, he fully realized that God is All, All is God.

He truly realized, during the closing hours of his vigil, that there is none separate from, or other than, God, the All, and that the All-Being is all there is to be. This is why, actually, Jesus was never on that cross, nor did he die on that cross. He did not need to come out from the sepulcher; he was never entombed there. He knew too much. He knew, and knows, what he is, has always been, and will always be. And this Christ-Man is what *you* are, all that you are, have ever been, and will ever be.

In our Bible, there is great significance in the two gardens. The first is the Garden of Eden, in which the Christ-Man is aware of being the Christ-Consciousness. He is aware of being in the Kingdom of Heaven and of *being* the Kingdom—Consciousness. Of course, the second garden referred to is the Garden of Gethsemene, where Jesus is supposed to have been betrayed, rejected, and to have suffered. The beautiful significance of this latter experience is the recognition that Jesus, the Christ, *had never actually left the Garden of Eden*. He did not really forget what he had always known, and known himself to be. It was only a "seeming." But the seeming never touched the Christ-Consciousness which was—and is—the only one they called Jesus. What then is the Resur-rection? It is the same kind of resurrection that each one of us seems to experience. Never can we forget what we have known, and known our Self to be.

It was no happenstance that our Bible was written. It had to be written. The Absolute Truth revealed in the Bible was the reason why it had to be recorded. The Truth is not true because we find it in the Bible. Rather, it is that we find this Truth in the Bible because It already existed before the Bible was written and had to be revealed in this Bible. True it is that this Truth seems to be concealed in many statements of this great Book. But when we read the Bible in full Light, these Truths cannot be concealed.

Chapter XVI

Immutability

As we have stated before, there is absolutely nothing that can change God, who is absolute, eternal, constant Perfection. That which is called human vision cannot change or lessen the Absolute Perfection that is all Substance, all Form, and all Activity. It is those of us who imagine that we are born beings who seem to see, hear, and experience imperfection. This is a paradox because all the while it seems that we are seeing, hearing, and experiencing falsely, we actually are hearing, seeing, and experiencing Absolute Perfection. There simply is no imperfection for us to know anything about at all. It is only that we appear to see, hear, and experience the perfect Substance imperfectly. Nonetheless, this perfect Substance remains unchanged, despite our seeming imperfect seeing, hearing, and experiencing of it.

Of course, it is all a matter of Consciousness, and Consciousness, being Absolute Perfection, can never be aware of seeing, hearing, or being imperfect. Thus, even our apparent "seeing" cannot change, alter, or diminish the Absolute Perfection which is All Substance.

So long as we seem to see bodies, objects, trees, etc., as imperfect, we are not seeing as perfect Vision. So long as we seem to see Substance in Form as ugly, distorted, etc., we are not seeing as perfect Vision. So long as we seem to see abnormality, decrepitude, and the like, we are seeing imperfectly. So long as we seem to see newborn babies, we are not seeing the Substance in Form that really is before us. In order to actually see the Body of anyone or anything, we must see It at the very height of completeness and Perfection. If the Body of one called a baby had to grow, to mature, and then decline or deteriorate, then we would have change. But God, being the Principle—Immutability—simply does not become a born baby body, then a child's body, a mature body, and then an old body.

In illumination, I have never seen a baby body, nor have I seen an aging or old body. Neither have I seen a distorted or ugly body. I am now speaking of the Body of the tree, the rose, or any Substance in Form. So long as we seem to see bodies that are solid matter, we are seeing imperfectly. It is futile to try to change Substance, Form, and Activity. We certainly can't improve that which is absolutely perfect already.

Every attempt we make to improve the Body by diet, exercise, drugs, etc., only seems to add to our imperfect seeing or to our misconception, in which we have imperfect vision of things as they are. There is never imperfect being. There only seems to be imperfect seeing, or perception. One day, all of us are going to see the futility of trying to make the body more perfect, and we will really see—perceive—and experience *being* the eternal, constant, immutable Body that we genuinely are.

Throughout the ages, man has been trying to improve a supposedly imperfect body. Even our friends, the Buddhistic yogis, have their breathing exercises, their bodily postures, etc. It is true that some of them are more interested in attaining illumination, and thus, Nirvana. But there are some who feel that these exercises and postures are of greater importance in "building" a better body. Jesus said, "According to your belief shall it be unto you." And because they *believe* in these exercises, often, to them, there does seem to be bodily improvement. But sooner or later, these supposed "better bodies" are going to seem to run down, to become aged and decrepit. Why is this true? Because the kind of body they are trying to improve simply does not exist.

There really is one Body and one kind of Body. The word *mankind* simply means a *kind* of man who begins to be alive, concious, etc., at birth, then becomes unalive and unconscious at death. But that kind of man does not exist. The only Man who does exist is the Christ-Man. And the only Body that does exist is the forever constant, changeless Christ-Body, or Body of the Christ.

The physicists claim that all substance remains the same substance but the forms constantly change in which this substance appears. For instance, they say that the tree falls to the earth and the substance of the tree deteriorates and becomes dust, etc. Thus, the substance of the tree is supposed to reappear in an entirely different Form. In a somewhat similar way, some branches of the Buddhist faith believe that man may begin as an insect, turtle, serpent, or substance in some lesser Form and finally change into the Form called man. This is a misconception of the Body of Man. The Form, Substance, and the Activity of this Body never has and never will change. Why is this true? The Form of every atom remains that Form and no other. The Form of every nucleus remains that Form. It simply cannot change. What is the atom? What is all Substance in Form? God. Isn't God All? Of course. What is the Substance in Form called the Body? God—and God does not change. Thus, the Substance, the Form, and Activity called this Body is forever immutable.

Now, in order to present this basic Truth as succinctly as possible, let us say it in this way: everything and everyone that we can possibly view, or see, is constantly, changelessly perfect because Perfection is all there is to see, to hear, or to be. But we, because we imagine ourselves to be temporary, ever changing, born man, *seem* to believe in, and see, our own fallacious picturization of our expectations. In short, we see what we believe, even as we believe what we see.

In our class in Vista in 1966, we perceived the fact that the ever-surging, circling universal Substance is manifested in, and as, countless Forms and Activity. We also realized that the Form of any Substance is also circling at that particular tempo. The Form cannot change because the rythmic tempo that is *that* Form cannot change. The rythmic tempo of any Activity remains the same rythmic tempo constantly and eternally. It is Absolute Perfection in action, being Substance, Activity, and Form. Now, what are we to realize in order that the eternal, immutable Perfection that *is* be evident as all that we see, all that we hear or experience?

First of all, we are to know what Vision is, what hearing is, and what changeless, perfect, eternal Being is. We are to know that there is one Vision and One who sees. Perfect seeing is perfect Vision *being*. Perfect seeing is Perfection seeing perfectly. It is conscious Perfection aware of being the Perfection that It sees. It is conscious Perfection being perfect Vision, *and you are that*.

We completely disregard so-called born eyes. We are unconcerned, whatever they may seem to see or as to how they seem to see. Rather, we just maintain our awareness of being eternal, constant, perfect Vision Itself in all of Its Perfection, Immutability, and Eternality. Oh, beloved One, the seeing, that which is seen, and the Being are all one and the same. *And you are that*. Never can you see anything outside of, or other than, the infinite Consciousness you are. And you are this Being, being everywhere. You *are* that which you see.

Right now, I would like to refer you to the chapter in *The Ultimate* entitled "Seeing is Being." Now much more will be revealed through the study and contemplation of this chapter.

Let us simply, and without effort, refuse to believe, acknowledge, or accept any appearance of change or of imperfection. Let us always be aware of the fact that whatever we are viewing or seeing is the Absolute Perfection that we are, and it is this Perfection being Substance, Form, and Activity. Let us also perceive the Fact that the *only* Vision that sees anything is the perfect Vision that we are, seeing only Perfection. It is Perfection aware of seeing and being Its everlasting, perfect, changeless Self. *And we are that Self.*

If we seem to see imperfection, our imperfect seeing would have to be imperfect being, or imperfection being. This is true because "Seeing is being." The Substance in Form that we see consists of the Consciousness that we *are*, being. Actually, it is the Consciousness that we are, aware of being. If, therefore, we seem to see imperfection, then we would only appear to be seeing (perceiving) and being our own Substance and Activity. Thus, we would have to be aware of being imperfect, or of being imperfection. This is true because seeing really is being. But since we only *seem* to see imperfection, what we appear to see is only a seeming. We would only seem to be seeing, thus being, our own perfect Substance as though It were imperfect substance, form, and activity. Yet it is all a "seeming" and nothing else. Therefore, if we appear to be seeing change and imperfection, we are not really seeing anything at all. It is all only an appearance, and an appearance is not the Substance in Form and Activity that really is the Something that really *is*.

But truly, we never see change or imperfection, for the only Vision that exists which can see anything at all is the immutable Perfection that is. It only sees Its own immutable, perfect Substance, Form, and Activity. This is Absolute Vision. This is Vision being Absolute. Of course, the same Truth that has just been revealed pertaining to Vision is also true of hearing. Actually, hearing and seeing are identical. Both hearing and seeing are the same Consciousness perceiving.

That which the so-called born ear of assumptive man hears, such as words of troubles, problems, etc., are only words expressed in noises, or sounds, produced by fallacious born man. Any words of criticism or condemnation are the same thing — sounds, or noises, expressed in words. Really, we come to a point where any words that pertain to assumptive born man, his human ambition, his self-glorification, etc., mean no more to us than would pebbles falling upon a tin pan. Any sounds of imperfection, supposedly emanating from this non-man, we simply do not hear. We don't believe them or accept them.

This so-called born man is neither good nor bad. He simply is nothing because there is no birth, thus, no born man.

Chapter XVII

Faith Is the Substance of Things Apparently Not Seen

What happens when a seeming healing takes place? Well, that which to supposedly born man seems invisible, unknowable, is perceived to be visible and knowable right here and now.That which appears to this suppositional man to be invisible and inexperiencable is seen and experienced. Earlier during this class experience, we announced that we might even perceive how it is that this apparently invisible Body could be, and would, be visible.

Now we have arrived at this point. What is the meaning of "Faith is the substance ... "? It means that faith is the Substance. It means that the Mind (Intelligence) that has, or is, absolute Faith in the Fact that the Substance in Form which *appears* to be invisible really is the only Substance. And it is this ever-living, conscious Mind that is the very Substance in Form which has been considered to be invisible.

But our Bible states, "there is nothing hidden that shall not be revealed" (Luke 8:17). This is a tremendous statement of Truth. It has far greater significance than we have previously realized. This statement proclaims the passing of the age-old illusion that the eternal, living Body must forever remain invisible. If it were true, we could never be through with the tragic illusion that death is inevitable. Thus, the promise in our Bible of the eternal Life would not be fulfilled. If we continue to accept this illusion that the perfect, eternal Body must forever remain invisible, we are surely going to continue to seem to die. And so long as we continue to imagine that Substance in Form is seen by supposedly born eyes, we are not really going to see the Substance that really is right here.

But the instant we see, know, and experience being the living, eternal, conscious Substance that is, we see, we know, and we experience being this Substance. Thus, the conscious, living Mind that is Absolute Faith in the seemingly invisible Substance really is this Substance in Form Itself. This I AM is the living Mind that is this very Substance, Form, and Activity that has appeared to be invisible. Thus, the Mind that is complete Faith in being the apparently unseen Substance—Body—really is the Substance in which It has Faith.

So when so-called bodily healing takes place, what Activity is going on? Beloved, the eternal, perfect Mind that is all Absolute Faith—or Self-knowledge—is seen, known, and experienced. Yes, It is experienced as the only Bodily Substance in existence. Thus, the apparently invisible Substance is actually visible. Furthermore, the seemingly unknown, eternal, perfect Body is experienced as a visible Substance. And they call it a healing.

When a supposed healing of something such as a goiter, a swollen or inflamed area, etc., takes place, it is evident that so-called healing has revealed visible Perfection right where imperfection seemed to be visible. In short, the Perfection that seemed to be invisible is visible. It is seen right here as the Substance of the one who had apparently been healed, and the imperfection which had seemed to be visible is perceived to be invisible—it is not seen as the Substance of the one who has apparently been healed. This, Beloved, is, something of tremendous significance. It will bear much study and contemplation.

You may wonder why the entire Body of the one who is apparently healed is not revealed as the Perfection it is. The answer is: *no one expects it or believes it to be possible.* Yet it *is* possible. I have seen it take place many times. At any rate, this so-called healing is an indication that the entire, eternal, perfect Body *can* be seen. It really is visible, and It is visible the very moment that we perceive It to be the only Body that is, that ever was, or that will ever be.

You see, we appear to have become bogged down and so enmeshed in the illusion of a temporary, changing body that we do not seem to see the Body that is. Why is this true? It is true because, throughout the ages, this false opinion has been handed down as Fact—the only Fact—and we seem to have been saddled with it. But it simply is not true. And now we are at the point of the great discovery, which is:

That which has always been believed to be a visible born body is not, and never was, the Body at all. And that Body which we have believed to be invisible, really is, and has always been, the *only* Body. As we have stated again and again, there are not two bodies. There is only one Body that you can have or be.

You see, the mistake has been that we have erroneously believed that Spirit, Soul, Life, Mind, inhabit a born body. But because Spirit seemed to be invisible, this eternal Substance could never be seen. Yet whenever a supposed healing of something imperfect is seen, we have seen the proof, the evidence, of the visible Perfection right where It had seemed to be invisible. What is the visible Perfection that *is*? Beloved, It is God, Spirit, Consciousness, Life, Mind, Love. So eternal, perfect, conscious, living, loving Mind (Intelligence*) is visible*.

Now, we can be assured that this same Truth is true as the *only* Activity that goes on in, and as, the bodily activity. It may seem that perfect Activity is absent. It may appear that the Activity that is present is imperfect activity. But the visible manifestation of perfect Activity may be seen and experienced at any moment.

Hence, we now have perceived perfect Substance, perfect Form, and now we are aware of perfect Activity, which is eternal, constant, and eternally, constantly active. I am not speaking merely of the Body that you are or that I am. I am speaking of the

Body of the bird, the Body of the butterfly, the leaf, a drop of water, the Body of everyone and everything. We simply *have* to perceive that all Substance that seems to be invisible truly is visible and that this apparently invisible Substance is the *only* Substance, Form, and Activity.

Why is this so necessary? The nuclear bomb has revealed the necessity that this Truth be perceived. So let our faith be Absolute in that which does not appear to be seen. Let our faith be completely in that which is called invisible. Let our faith be so steady, so constant, and so unwavering that the seemingly unseen is seen, felt, and experienced. Thus, the apparently invisible *is* visible, and we see, know, and experience *being* the evidence of that upon which our faith has stood.

As you know, the title of this chapter refers to a quotation from Hebrews. Now, let us turn to the complete quotation:

> Now, faith is the substance of things hoped for, the evidence of things not seen" (Heb. 11:1).

We do hope for the evidence of the Perfection that seems to be invisible and unknown. If we did not innately feel that Perfection is at least possible, we would not hope for perfect Substance, Form, and Activity to be visibly evidenced. So not one of us is completely devoid of faith in the apparently invisible Perfection. Even assumptive born man—if such there were—is not so steeped in the miasma of illusion that he does not, to some extent, realize the Truths we have been seeing, and it is this very fact that brings forth the evidence. It is this inherently felt Truth that evidences Itself as the eternal, constant, perfect Substance, which really has been the *only* visible Presence all the while. Mind is Substance. And the Mind that has—or is—faith is the very Substance, Form, and Activity of that which seems to be—but is not—invisible. This is the Substance hoped for but apparently unseen, or evidenced

Now let us more fully discuss this subject of Substance. What is the substance of things hoped for? The words *Mind* and *Consciousness* are synonomous. Conscious Mind is all Substance. Intelligent Consciousness is all Substance. Conscious, intelligent Life is all Substance, so all Substance is alive, or an ever-living Substance. The words *Mind, Consciousness, Life,* and *Love* are synonomous. So intelligent, living Love is all Substance.

Again, what is this "substance of things hoped for"? What is this apparently unseen Substance? It is Consciousness, or awareness of being. It is your very Consciousness that you exist. The Consciousness that you *are*, aware that you exist, is the only Substance in existence: This is the only Substance there is, so it has to be the Substance you have and that you are.

Oh, beloved One, do you see what this means? It means that the Consciousness you are aware of being is the Substance that comprises Infinity, or the

Universe Itself. You now perceive that you simply cannot be a temporary, born, perishable, human body.

There is but *one* Being. There is not another. And this is God, the Universe, Being. Thus, It cannot be a separate human being.

Chapter XVIII

Supply Is Substance

Your God I AM Consciousness of being, or the Consciousness of being that you are, *is* the Substance of every galaxy, every star, and planet. You are the Substance and the Activity of the planet Earth—its valleys and its mountains; its oceans, lakes, and rivers; the rain and the sands of the wonderful desert. All, All, All is the awareness of being that you are.

Now, what then, can you lack? Could money be absent from your awareness of being? Isn't your awareness of being the very presence, the essence, of all that is called money? Isn't this your Consciousness that you exist? How far are you from this Consciousness? Does it seem you lack a home? Aren't you the very Essence of the Substance, Form, and Activity that is that home? Can you lack Love, when you *are* Love? Can anything or anyone be missing from your Completeness, from your complete awareness that you exist? It is all Consciousness; it is all God; it is all the very Consciousness of being that *you* are. No matter what may seem to be missing from your awareness of being, it is well to ask your God I AM Self just such questions as the foregoing. You will marvel at the further revelations and the visible evidence of the "substance of things hoped for."

Now, we know that the Consciousness that has faith, that has absolute conviction in being the Substance that is eternal, constant, ever-perfect, *is* the Substance in which It has faith. This is the Substance of the tree that never grew from the seed in the ground. This is the Substance of the rose that never had to be planted in the earth. And this is the Substance of the Christ-Man who never had to be conceived and born in order to be.

This, Beloved, is why there is no death. Not a flower fades and dies. Not a tree falls and perishes. Not a butterfly disappears and ends. Why is this true? It is a positive Fact because nothing — *absolutely nothing* — that exists had a beginning. And of course, this is why it is impossible that Man should die. Why? Because Man never began, thus Man cannot end.

The birthless, deathless
Christ-Man is the *only* Man.

Chapter XIX

Seeing Is Perceiving

You realize that in our general use of the word *see* we mean to perceive. Seeing *is* perception. In our Bible, the words *see* or *seeing* are sometimes used in this way. For instance, we read the expression "seeing through a glass, darkly" or "now we see in part, then face to face." Again, we read, "We shall see him as he is." In 1 John 3:2, we read:

> Beloved, now are we the sons of God, and it doth not yet appear what we shall be: but we know that when he shall appear, we shall be like him; for we shall see him as he is.

Isn't this a wonderful statement of Truth? Of course, now we know that the Father is the Son, even as the Son is the Father. And it is so true that in order to see God, the so-called little "I" must be completely transcended. But once we do really *see* God, we have literally seen all there is of our God I AM Self. Someone has said that if you wish to see God, look into the face of Man, and this is Absolute Truth. But it is also true that if we wish to see Man, we must look into the face of God. The face of God *is* the face of Man, even as the face of Man is the face of God. And we are more than like God. There is one Being—God—and we *are* that one God, Being.

There is another aspect of Truth that should be revealed here. Again and again, we have mentioned the fact that there is no born man, thus, no born body. Now, it should be pointed out that this revelation does not mean a denial of the Body. This would be a mistake. Of course, we never deny anything. But above all, no one should ever deny the Body. Instead of a denial of this wonderful.Body, we have full faith in Its eternal, perfect, intelligent Substance. Even before the supposedly invisible Body is seen, our faith is in the apparently invisible Body. But what about the born body?

Well, now we know there really is no born body. So why deny something that does not even exist? We don't. The secret is in the fact that we have no faith in a born body. Our entire faith is in the eternal unborn Body, and as far as we are concerned, anything that has no existence does not exist for us. But the constant, unborn, perfect Body is real to us. It is genuine. And this is why, finally, we do see this Body. It is visible.

Often we see many Bodies and many varieties of Body, and it is possible for us to reach a point where we can see every Body as It is, almost constantly. This experience, Beloved, is seeing God face to face. Oh, if something that claims to be imperfect keeps prodding at our Consciousness and claiming our attention, we do not ignore it. We just say something like:

>   Oh, I don't believe that. What is that to the *I*
>   that I am and that everyone is? I know what I am.
>   I am what I know. That which I am, this one and
>   everyone is. What this one and everyone is, I am.

Just something like that is sufficient. It is all so simple. Why make a problem of it? But we never deliberately deny the Body or anything else. After a while, we find that our attention simply cannot be diverted from the conscious Perfection that *is*. Then we find that there isn't even an *appearance* of anything other than the infinite, eternal Perfection that we are. So now, whenever our attention is focalized as Body, it is always on the one and *only* Body, and it would never occur to us that there could be another Body.

I AM Is My Name

> I am the Heaven and the Earth,
> Eternal Life that knows no birth,
> No sorrow, suffering, pain.
> I am the Life that knows no death,
> No change, no one to be bereft
> Of ones so dear.
> The Life I am is ever here,
> completely free from loss or fear;
> forevermore the same,
> for I AM is my Name.

Right in front of my study window stands a huge eucalyptus tree. I have written about this tree before, so I shall not repeat that which has already been published. Many of you have seen this tree, however, and you have seen that the visible Body of this tree actually glows, The Light that *is* this tree shines right through the appearance of solidity, revealing clearly the Body of Light. Right here, you have seen the seemingly invisible Substance in Form because you have seen the Light which is the genuine and only Body of this tree. True it is that to a few of you the tree appears to be solid, even though all of you do see the Light shining through the apparent solidity. However, some of you have seen the Body of the tree as pure Light through and through. Well, we are coming closer to the Absolute Fact pertaining to the seemingly invisible being undeniably visible.

We know that Jesus could and did appear to most of those around him as a solid, born human body. But on the Mount of Transfiguration, he revealed his Body to be pure Light, and It was visible. In fact, at that moment It was the *only* Body that was visible. We also know that when it seemed wisdom to do so, Jesus simply put off the material appearance of body. Of course, whatever Jesus did—or does—always means a fulfillment of a definite purpose is involved. You know that when the throng wished to seize him, suddenly he was invisible right in the midst of them. We also know that though no one saw him cross the water, he was seen on the other side of the lake. All of this took place right in the midst of the crowds around him.

Did his Body really disappear? Of course not. If It had, he would have been, at least temporarily, bodiless, and this is impossible. All that happened was that the so-called born eyes of those around him could not see Jesus at all. Furthermore, Jesus knew that because he was, and is, the indivisible Christ-Consciousness, his Body could be seen wherever and whenever it was necessary for the fulfillment of a definite purpose.

Now, the following statement may seem shocking, but please bear with me until it also has fulfilled its purpose. *Our Body can also be seen wherever and whenever it is necessary for the fulfillment of some definite purpose for It to be seen.*

Now, if the Body were always invisible, we would never be able to appear as a visible Body to those who seem to need to see us. For instance, suppose that Jesus had never appeared on this planet as a visible Body. Would that have been Love in action? Would it have fulfilled the glorious purpose for which Jesus became visible? Of course not.

In like manner, if someone seems desperate and petrified by fear, his need to see a visible Body does seem to be very great. In just such a case as this, our Body will definitely be seen. More often than not, we are not even aware of this fact. We simply "feel" a cry for help, and the loving Christ-Consciousness that we are fulfills Its purpose in the way that is necessary at the moment.

Actually, everything that ever takes place is a fulfillment of purpose. Not long ago I read an article by one of the leading astrophysicists in which he stated that in studying this Universe he was amazed at how purposeful It is. He definitely stated that this a purposeful Universe. I have also talked with highly respected medical men who have said the very same thing about the Body. All Activity is purposeful, and Its purpose is always fulfilled. Right here is where that word *Mind* is important. As is often stated, this is an intelligent Universe. Mind is Intelligence, and if there were no Intelligence, the entire Universe would be in chaos, if indeed It still existed.

It seemed necessary at the moment to include this short intersperse. But let us now continue with our subject. We were speaking of the necessity for Body that seems to be invisible to be visible when a purpose is to be fulfilled in this way.

It is possible that we can see *all* Substance, Form, and Activity as It *is*, rather than as It is not. Oh yes, this is happening right today. Many of you who are veterans in the Absolute Ultimate have seen, and do see, this *inhabited* kingdom of God which is right here and now. *This is Heaven, and when we truly see it, we know, and we know that we know.*

So long as we, at the moment, seem to be generally focalized here on this planet Earth, let us consider this planet as it is. To really *see* this planet is to marvel at the Perfection, Peace, and Beauty it is. It really is gloriously beautiful. There never is a sign of imperfection. There are no troubled faces. There is only the Beauty of Perfection and the Perfection that is Beauty. There is no sign of age or deterioration. There is not one barren branch; no, not even one dead or dying blade of grass. Oh, it is wonderful.

Many of you have seen this kingdom that is right here. Just at first, some of you have imagined that you were seeing Life as it is on some other planet. Then you realized that what you were seeing was really this planet right here — but not the way you had seen it prior to this glorious experience. Well, you have merely seen Life and all existence right here as it is, as it has always been, and as it will eternally be.

If there were not many of you who have already experienced the Truth of the following statement, I should certainly hesitate to make it: we are the Power to be visible to anyone, whenever and wherever it is the fulfillment of a purpose for us to be seen. At once, though, I must add that we do not do anything to make ourselves visible. It is exceedingly important that this point be crystal clear. You see, the purpose and the fulfillment of the purpose are Mind (Intelligence) in action, and of course, this is God, Consciousness, Life, and above all, *Love*.

Again and again, someone has called and said, "I called upon God, and suddenly you were standing right here beside me." Well, of course — God is the Christ-Consciousness, even as the Christ-Consciousness is God. The Christ-Consciousness is indivisibly *One*. Every one of us is the Christ-Consciousness. Thus, when anyone calls upon God, the Christ-Consciousness, he has only called upon the Consciousness that he is. And because some purpose is being fulfilled here, in this experience, whomever should appear does appear visibly. It is as simple as that. We never have any awareness of doing anything, or of trying to do anything, in this experience.

When we perceive that we are visibly present anywhere, we simply perceive that we are visibly there. However, it is never "there" as far as we are concerned. Always it is "here." Whenever we find ourself visibly focalized anywhere, it is always "here" to us. Of course, this is true because all of us are the Christ-Consciousness that is constantly and eternally *everywhere*. It is only when the fulfillment of purpose requires the visible Body to appear that It does appear. Jesus, the Christ, has visibly appeared to innumerable Identities who have called upon the Christ.

Are we not the very same Christ-Consciousness that exists as Jesus the Christ? Of course. What other Consciousness could we be, when there *is no other Consciousness*? We are supremely unlimited. Nothing limits us. We only seem to limit ourselves because we go right on deluding ourselves that we are born human beings. Once we transcend that miasma, *all things are possible to us*.

Beloved, let us see just what all of this means in our everyday, practical experience. It means that anything we seem to need is here right now and is visible. And the practical evidence of its presence may be seen, and will be seen, exactly when it fulfills its purpose in and as our experience. It matters not whether the seeming need be for a home, a friend, money, or whatever. This Truth is true and it proves Itself to be true. I have literally seen someone whom I had not met until I had seen that one in contemplation. I also know those who have seen an employer before they had met or become employed by that one. Oh yes, offices, studios, homes, etc., have been seen before ever buying, renting, or even entering them.

Do you ask how this can be? It can be — and it is possible for any one of us to experience, the very moment that we stop limiting oursselves to the little so-called born man's misconception of himself. We can stop doing this right here and now. But we won't stop so long as we cling to birth as though it were genuine.

What is the difference between these Identities we see before we meet them and the Identity when we do meet him? What is the difference between the offices, houses, etc., when we foresee them and the offices and houses in which we later work or live? None at all. It is only that the later experience is fulfilling its purpose in our daily affairs. But the house in which the Identity actually lives no more consists of solid matter than was the house he saw prior to the actual practical experience. Where was the house? Where was the office? It existed in, and as, the I Am Consciousness of the one who had the experience.

Everyone and everything that is necessary to your steady fulfillment of purpose is present here and now as your Consciousness. This, Beloved, is why there can be no such thing as a prophecy. You see, prophecy interprets everything as something that is to take place at some supposed future time. Since everyone and everything already *is*, there can be nothing that is going to *become* something. Neither can there be an experience that is not present right here and now in, and as, your Consciousness. The following quotation states this Fact very clearly:

> The thing that has been, it is that which shall be: and that which is done, is that which shall be done: and there is no new thing under the sun (Eccles. 1:9).

Now we can perceive why we are never going to be any more perfect, anymore successful, or any happier than we are right now. It is all present and actively fulfilling Its purpose in, and as, the Consciousness that we are. Isn't this a wonderful thing to realize? And we can now clearly see that there is neither time nor space.

All is. All is being now.

Chapter XX

Beyond All Limitations

Inherently, Man knows that the seeming limitations foisted upon him are unnecessary and abnormal. Throughout the centuries, he has resisted them and made every attempt to dispose of them. But we have to recognize the fact that these so-called limitations are due to assumptive man's acceptance of them and an almost determined effort, for the most part, to cling to them. But among those who insist upon clinging to these pseudo limitations, there are always those of greater and clearer vision, those who refuse to accept them or be governed by them. Such a one was Columbus. Of course, he was not the first one who refused to be limited. But we are so familiar with his so-called historic feat, that we will begin with him.

We know the doubts and the fears that attempted to stop this adventure into the seeming unknown. We know the seeming ignorance, or darkness, of those who opposed his sailing. Oh, they were so sure that the ships would sail right over the edge of a flat world, a type of world which did not even exist. Nonetheless, Columbus did arrive at a destination far greater than he had envisioned.

Right here is an important record of Man's refusal to accept the so-called limitations of that which is called space. Since then, there have continued to be those who have refused to be bound by the limitations of suppositional space. But this is not all. More and more rapidly, Man has been obliterating the seeming limitations of that which is called time. But of course, the two assumptions called space and time are really one, and it was impossible for assumptive space to be transcended without also the transcendence of so-called time.

Charles Lindbergh is a wonderful example of one who refused to be limited by so-called space and time, and since his historic flight, the obliteration of the limitation of supposed space and time has moved with increasing rapidity.

Now, of course, we know our wonderful astronauts reveal ever greater proof that there are no so-called limitations where supposed space and time are concerned. Of course, many there were who said, "It can't be done." And many there were who said that never would we land a man on the moon, and if we did so, he would never be able to get off the moon. Well, Man will prove the fallacy of these so-called limitations, and this, Beloved, will be followed by ever greater proofs of the limitless, spaceless, timeless Universe.

We are moving along so rapidly in the obliteration of the illusion of time and space that no doubt the actual fact of this matter will soon be perceived. What is this fact?

> Man does not have to go anywhere in order to consciously be anywhere that is his fulfillment of purpose.

Oh, there are many of us who are aware of this fact. It is never a matter of traveling or going anywhere. Neither is it a matter of projecting one's Self to any given area. It is not even a matter of desire or a decision to be at any given locale. It is just that suddenly we are there, but as stated before, always it is *here*. Wherever you are aware of being is always here.

Now, where is space and what is space? There is no space. And what about time? What about the so-called time it would take to travel to Mars, to Venus, or to Timbuktu? Instantaneous, conscious presence anywhere reveals that there is no time. So much for the so-called limitations of that which is called time and space.

But there are—or seem to be—so many ways in which we appear to limit ourselves. For instance, we have largely accepted the persuasion that Life is a limited, temporary experience extending between that which is called birth and that which is called death. I believe the Bible states that we are allotted some seventy years. Well, we do not have to be bound by such limitations, and there are some of us who refuse to bow down to such bondage.

It is noteworthy that, all the while, the medical profession has been attempting to prolong this so-called period in which man is supposed to be permitted to live, and they are meeting with some measure of success. But just as is the case with the astronauts in their courageous attempts to obliterate so-called time and space, so it is with the medical profession. Laudible it is indeed, but it is never enough. It is not, and cannot be, the complete answer. Now let us perceive what is the answer.

The answer lies in the revelation that all Life is eternal, beginningless, changeless, and endless. The answer lies in the fact that birth is a misconception and that death is but this same misconception expanded. The so-called life they are trying to prolong is supposed to be a life that is born. But actually, Life is never born. This, Beloved, is why Life can never die.

When revelation is complete where Life is concerned, there will be no more *seeming* death. And when the eternal, ever-enduring Body is perceived as It *is*, there will no more be an appearance of a body that is supposed to be born or to die. This is the complete answer. It is all revelation. But as often stated, all revelation is Self-revelation. *You* are the Self that is to experience the revelation *to* the Self, *as* the eternal everlasting *Self*. In this way only will the so-called limitation of Life Itself be transcended.

Let us now consider another *apparent* limitation to which we seem to be in bondage. We are supposedly allotted just so many years in which to be in perfect, or at least good, health. Then a gradual deterioration is supposed to begin and to continue until the final so-called enemy overtakes us. Now, God *is* Love, but there certainly is no Love in such an edict. Love could never be so cruel. But to continue, it seems that, for the most part, we have accepted this cruel deception. And of course, we have appeared to be bound by its inflexibility.

Who made such decisions for us? Whoever made such cruel so-called laws and placed us in bondage to them? *These are not laws — they are merely opinions of assumptive man.* But we are *not* assumptive man. Actually, there is no assumptive man, and certain it is that we are not in bondage to so-called laws of a kind of man that does not even exist. We are not limited to just a short period of harmony, joy, and Perfection. Heaven is here and now. Never have we left Heaven. How could we, when Heaven is our own Consciousness? Therefore, we are not bound by the so-called limitations of assumptive man.

Oh, there are innumerable ways in which we seem to accept the limitations of mankind, or a kind of man who does not exist. That which follows presents just a few of these spurious limitations, and perhaps this presentation will alert us to many other impositions of these limiting falsities.

For instance, we are supposed to have eight hours of sleep every night. Otherwise, our efficiency is supposed to be affected and even our health jeopardized. Again and again, this fallacy has proved to be sheer fantasy, yet most of us continue to accept it and to be limited by it. Then there is the so-called limitation concerning food. It is generally believed that we must have so many vitamins of various kinds in order to be maintained in good health. Our very strength is supposed to be dependent upon what we eat or drink. Now, are we really dependent upon food and drink for our Perfection, our strength, our very Life? Is God the only Life, or is there another and more powerful Life? We know the answer to that.

Now, of course, no one can *compel* himself to see through these so-called limitations, and no one should try to deliberately break through them. It would be futile and a mistake to do so. But each one of us should be alert to them. And there will come a day when revelation will reveal the absolute freedom from the seeming bondage of all limitations.

It has to be revelation, identification, and manifestation. There is no other way. In the meantime, let us recognize the fallacy of all limitations and be full open for the glorious revelation that always we have been completely free from all limitations; always we will be free from this apparent bondage; and right now, whether or not it appears to be true, we *are* completely free from any bondage of any nature. Why? Because we are Infinitude—God, the All—being Completeness Itself. And this Completeness means that we are the Principle which is complete freedom. Thus it is, Beloved.

> Consider these Absolute Truths
> because *you* are these Truths.

Chapter XXI

Self-Revelation

In the latter section of the Book of Revelation, we find some statements which are not really prophecies at all. They are exactly what they are called in the Bible—that is, *revelation*. Now, all revelation is *Self*-revelation, so genuinely speaking, they are the Self-revelations of every one of us. These statements are not revelations of things to come. Rather, they are absolute statements of things that already constantly and eternally *are*. This is nothing more nor less than Consciousness perceiving, Consciousness being, just what It *is* and *All* that It is.

> And I saw a new heaven and a new earth: for the first heaven and the first earth were passed away ... and I heard a great voice out of heaven saying, Behold the tabernacle of God is with man, and he will dwell with them, and they shall be his people, and God himself shall be with them, and be their God.

> And God shall wipe away all tears from their eyes; and there shall be no more death, neither sorrow, nor crying, neither shall there be any more pain: for the former things are passed away.

> And he that sat upon the throne said, Behold, I make all things new ... And he said unto me, It is done. I am Alpha and Omega, the beginning and

the end. I will give unto him that is athirst the fountain of the water of life freely" (Rev. 21:1, 3-6).

Here are wonderful statements of the Fact that when all misconception of beginning and ending is transcended, all former illusions of darkness are dissolved, and the only Substance in Form will be seen as it is—Light, Light, Light.

Then, in the next chapter, we find the key to the entire portrayal:

> And they shall see his face; and his name shall be in their foreheads. And there shall be no night there; and they shall need no candle, neither light of the sun; for the Lord God giveth them light: and they shall reign forever and ever" (Rev. 22:4-5).

Oh, there is such glorious Truth revealed in these few statements. Just for a moment, let us realize the importance of the statement "his name shall be in their foreheads." His name is I AM, which is the I AM that *you* are. When God says, "I am," He is not identifying Himself. Rather, He is making a statement of *being*. He is simply saying, "I am. I exist; therefore, I am. I am; therefore, I exist. I am aware of being. I am Being." And this, Beloved, is our "I am."

When we say "I am," we are not identifying ourselves. We are making a statement of being, of the fact that we exist. This is all that is necessary. "I am. I exist." And the full realization of all that these words *I am* mean is the Light itself. It really performs what the world calls miracles. "I am. All that God is, I am."

This is our statement of being the Principle Itself. This is our statement of being all Absolute Truth, or Principle. Then we can joyously proclaim:

> Would I be perfect? I am Perfection. Would I be eternal? I am Eternality. Would I be peaceful? I am Peace. Would I be joyous? I am Joy. Would I be intelligent? I am Intelligence, Mind. Would I have Life? I am Life. Would I be conscious? I am Consciousness. Would I be loving? I am Love. I have to be that which I am, for there is nothing else, or other, that I can be.

Often Jesus spoke in parables. We do have to look beyond the words in order that the seemingly secret revelations be perceived. Always in reading the Bible, it is necessary to be full open for the Truth behind and beyond the words.

Now, let us turn again to these verses from the Bible and let the Truths behind and beyond the words reveal themselves as the very Consciousness that we are.

"And I saw a new heaven and a new earth ..." Here John is really saying, "I see the Heaven that is this Earth. All is new. All is constant newness."

"... for the former things are passed away."

All the delusions of darkness are completely transcended, and the everlasting Kingdom—Consciousness—that is God is revealed to be all that is present. Let our Consciousness be full open. Let *us* see the Earth, the Heavens, all that the Universe includes as It *is*. Here and now, all is Light and there is no darkness at all. Wars, hatreds, so-called human frailties, are unknown. All is peace, joy, Perfection, ecstasy, *Love*.

There is so much Absolute Truth to be perceived in the six verses of Revelation quoted in full earlier that I sincerely hope you will study and contemplate them much, as full open Consciousness. It would be impossible to write all there is to be seen in these verses. Then, too, why should I seem to rob you of the glorious Self-revelations by putting them in the words that come as the Consciousness that I am?

Yes, God hath given us His name, I AM.

Chapter XXII

Transcendence Complete

If there were such a thing as death, that which is called birth would be the first death. That which is called the Resurrection is the complete transcendence above and beyond the miasma of this supposed first death, called birth. Those of us who transcend this suppositional first death right here, in the midst of apparent dualism, *know* there is no second death. Thus, for us it does not exist. This Truth is beautifully recorded in Revelation 20:16:

> Blessed and holy is he who hath part in the first resurrection: on such the second death hath no power.

The city that lieth foursquare, mentioned in Revelation 21:16, is the full and complete transcendence beyond all the limitations of so-called born man. Here the boundless Infinitude is perceived to be All *as* All. Infinite, inseparable Consciousness is revealed as the Consciousness of each and every one of us.

> And the city lieth foursquare, and the length is as large as the breadth ... The length and the breadth and the height of it are equal.

In this full transcendence, there are no temples—churches—no priests, ministers, masters, leaders, or teachers. Neither is there any organization. Completely beyond and above all duality, there is no "twoness" and no "otherness." Complete transcendence is the complete Light, and in this Light there is no darkness at all. Beyond all duality is the Lamb, which is pure Truth. Free from all impurity is the Light, and *we are that*.

In Revelation 21:22-23, this Absolute Truth is beautifully stated:

> And I saw no temple therein: for the Lord God Almighty and the Lamb are the temple of it. And the city had no need of the sun, neither of the moon, to shine in it: for the glory of God did lighten it, and the Lamb is the light thereof.

Yes, the pure Absolute Truth *is* the Light.

Having completely transcended all duality, we now are aware of the Fact that *we are the Absolute Truth*. Here we are beyond all fear, all trouble, pain, sorrow, or worry. We are completely free from all bondage. We walk in the Light *as* the Light. We walk in Absolute Freedom because we know that we are the Principle — Freedom — Itself. In Revelation 21:25, we find a graphic and powerful illustration of our complete transcendence beyond and above all dualism:

> And the gates of it shall not be shut at all by day: for there shall be no night there.

And so, Beloved, in the words of the Ultimate:

> We walk *in* the Light, *as* the Light, for we *are* the Light in which we walk.

Now we *know* that the beginning and the ending are one and the same. We know that where the beginning is supposed to be, there is also supposed to be the ending. But God being eternal and God being All, there can be no beginning. Neither can there be an ending. The circle is complete, and there is nowhere in or as this complete circle where there is either beginning or ending.

In Revelation 22:13, God is revealed as being the Beginning and the Ending. And because God is eternally, constantly omnipresent, there can be neither beginning nor ending:

> I am Alpha and Omega, the beginning and the end, the first and the last.

And because all is eternal, there can be neither first nor last. Oh, truly, God is All—All is God. And *we* are That.

The Infinite *I* That I Am

> And now, Beloved, the words are here,
> Poor vessels, it is true;
> And yet we speak them, free from fear,
> For they are ever new.
> The vibrant, glowing, living Light
> That *is*, beyond the words
> Is shining through, so pure, so bright,
> So clear it must be heard
> And seen and felt and known to be
> the *I* that is Infinity.

About the Author

During early childhood, Marie S. Watts began questioning: "Why am I? What am I? Where is God? What is God?"

After experiencing her first illumination at seven years of age, her hunger for the answers to these questions became intensified. Although she became a concert pianist, her search for the answers continued, leading her to study all religions, including those of the East.

Finally, ill and unsatisfied, she gave up her profession of music, discarded all books of ancient and modern religions, kept only the Bible, and went into virtual seclusion from the world for some eight years. It was out of the revelations and illuminations she experienced during those years, revelations that were sometimes the very opposite of what she had hitherto believed, that her own healing was realized.

During all the previous years, she had been active in helping others. After 1957, she devoted herself exclusively to the continuance of this healing work and to lecturing and teaching. Revelations continually came to her, and these have been set forth in this and every book.

To all seekers for Truth, for God, for an understanding of their own true Being, the words in her books will speak to your soul.

Made in the USA
Coppell, TX
02 September 2022

82495884R10111